Tectonic Shifts in Financial Markets

Henry Kaufman

Tectonic Shifts in Financial Markets

People, Policies, and Institutions

Henry Kaufman
New York, USA

ISBN 978-3-319-48386-3   ISBN 978-3-319-48387-0   (eBook)
DOI 10.1007/978-3-319-48387-0

Library of Congress Control Number: 2016959962

Cover illustration: © Brothers_Art, iStock / Getty Images Plus

Printed on acid-free paper

This Palgrave Macmillan imprint is published by Springer Nature
The registered company is Springer International Publishing AG
The registered company address is: Gewerbestrasse 11, 6330 Cham, Switzerland

For Sidney Homer and Marcus Nadler

Preface by Paul Volcker[1]

Former Chairman of the United States Federal Reserve

I have known Henry Kaufman for nearly six decades. As I thought about my relationship with Henry during all these years, I thought that I brought certain advantages to our friendship. I am older than Henry by six weeks. I am taller than Henry by twelve inches. And to my memory—maybe his memory is different—when we first met, at the Federal Reserve Bank of New York fifty-nine years ago, in my opinion, I outranked him by a little bit.

But if that is true, I also know that Henry is smarter, because he came to the Federal Reserve with more degrees than I had. He had a Ph.D. in economics before that degree became a mathematical degree. It was real economics at that stage. He has reflected his interests and his scholarship in writing four books, including this one. I once wrote half a book, so he has generated eight times what I've generated.

[1] Mr. Volcker originally delivered a version of this text as "Henry Kaufman: Speaking his Mind, Making the Country Better" at the Foreign Policy Association in New York on Dec. 6. 2011, when I was presented with the Foreign Policy Association Statesman Award. It is reprinted here with the permission of the Foreign Policy Association.

I know he is a generous man. He supports more educational institutions than I have attended, with a professorship here, and a building there, and all the rest. The most important fact that I can tell you is that Henry knows more about interest rates than I do. Now that may surprise you. How do I know this? There is a small book—696 pages—called *A History of Interest Rates* that covers Babylonian times through Wall Street. No, Henry did not write this book, but Henry has read it. I know Henry has read it for two reasons: He wrote a Foreword to the book. I have the new edition, and I know Henry and I know that he would not write a preface to a book if he had not read the new chapters. And Henry was very familiar with the first edition, which goes back some years. It was only 394 pages at that point. But in reading the preface to the book, I want to tell you why I know he knows all about interest rates.

He himself said, "My first examination of the history of interest rates was at the first edition." He had just taken a new job with Sidney Homer, who was the principal author of the book, at Salomon Brothers. Henry was instructed by Sidney to read the book, and I quote Henry, "in a meticulous way. I read every page out loud to my secretary, and it has made an imprint on my career." Truer words, I suspect, were never spoken.

You may know in many ways we have followed parallel careers for fifty-nine years. We actually grew up quite close together, about five miles apart geographically, but it was a lot more than five miles apart culturally. I grew up in a nice, white, suburban New Jersey. My family was the epitome of middle class Americana at that point. Henry and his family, who ended up only five miles away across the George Washington Bridge, were refugees from Nazi Germany. His experience was quite different from my experience, a little more exciting if truth be told. He ended up in Washington Heights, which was kind of a hotbed of talent at that point, fertilized in considerable part by refugees from Nazi Germany. Henry went, I think, to the same high school as Henry Kissinger. This was a place where refugees and their children somehow became citizens of the United States of America.

Back when I was in grammar school, we learned about George Washington, silver dollars thrown across the Rappahannock, cherry trees cut down, log cabins for Abe Lincoln, and on and on—all part of our kind of mythical history. Henry and his compatriots in Washington Heights must have missed all that. But what is interesting is that in a very short time, they became Americans. I don't know why Henry ended up with a true blue New York accent and Henry Kissinger never got over his German accent. But be that as it may, I think that it is really a source of pride for America that these people could be absorbed into the society of New York and make the contributions they have made.

I have to say, looking at Henry's career and some of the parallels we've had, that he no doubt loves his country. But he is also aware of its faults, not least in financial markets, and not so coincidentally in recent years. Henry is a man who grew up in our financial markets.

He started out in the Federal Reserve, went to Salomon, left after several years there, and has been an entrepreneur in the financial world. He is very aware of what has been going on, and he is as concerned as anybody about defaults and distresses in our economy and in our financial system. I think it is fair to say that, cognizant of all those problems, Henry wants to do something about it. He is aware of the problems: that's part of the reason he wrote his books. One of the important lessons of Henry's books is the degree to which those in financial markets have lost their way. Have they lost their sense of fiduciary responsibilities? Where is a sense of responsibility to the customer? Where is a sense of responsibility to an institution—the kind of institution and partnership that he grew up in—whether private or public? And where is the sense of personal responsibility among all the mechanistic, mathematical markets that exist in financial markets these days?

I don't know the answer to all those questions, but I do know that Henry Kaufman is still at it. He is speaking his mind and doing what he can do—intellectually, publicly, privately—to make this country better as a great American citizen.

Acknowledgments

As with two of my previous two books, David Sicilia, a professor of business and financial history at the University of Maryland, played an indispensable role as developmental editor on this project. He contributed to its conceptualization and cohesiveness. I continue to marvel at his erudition—the vast scope of his knowledge in the history of economics, business and financial markets. His thoughtful demeanor and encouragement helped rescue me from occasional blockages in thought and writing. For all of this I am very grateful.

Helen Katcher, my chief assistant for half a century, helped see me through this project and every other since my early days at Salomon Brothers. I cannot imagine a more loyal, steady, and patient right-hand woman.

I am also grateful to Peter Rup and Tom Klaffky for their help in compiling data for several of the figures in this book.

Contents

About the Author

Henry Kaufman is President of Henry Kaufman & Company, Inc., an economic and financial consulting firm established in 1988. For the previous twenty-six years, he was with Salomon Brothers Inc., where he served as Managing Director and Member of the Executive Committee, and led the firm's four research departments. He was also a Vice Chairman of the parent company, Salomon Inc. Before joining Salomon Brothers, Dr. Kaufman worked in commercial banking and served as an economist at the Federal Reserve Bank of New York.

Born in Germany in 1927, Henry Kaufman received a B.A. in economics from New York University in 1948; an M.S. in finance from Columbia University in 1949; and a Ph.D. in banking and finance from New York University Graduate School of Business Administration in 1958. He also received an honorary Doctor of Laws degree from New York University in 1982, and honorary Doctor of Humane Letters degrees from Yeshiva University in 1986 and from Trinity College in 2005.

Invited to speak before many leading economic and finance organizations around the world, Dr. Kaufman was three times designated one of the thirty most influential Americans by *U.S. News & World Report*. In 2001, the National Association for Business Economics conferred on him its prestigious Adam Smith Award. He is author of three previous books: *Interest Rates, the Markets, and the New Financial* World (1986)—which won the Columbia Business School's George S. Eccles Prize for excellence in economic writing; *On Money and Markets, A Wall Street Memoir* (2000); and *The Road to Financial Reformation* (2009).

Dr. Kaufman has supported higher education, intellectual freedom, and the arts as a philanthropist and as Trustee and former Chairman at the Institute of International Education; former Chairman of the Board of Overseers of New York University's Stern School of Business; Life Trustee of New York University and The Jewish Museum; Trustee of the Norton Museum of Art; Board Member of Tel-Aviv University; and Honorary Trustee and former President of The Animal Medical Center. He has endowed centers, chairs, and fellowships at several major universities. With his wife, Elaine, Dr. Kaufman has been a major benefactor of the Kaufman Music Center in New York City.

List of Figures

1

How It Began at Salomon Brothers

On the eve of the 1960s, even the most astute observers of financial markets had little inkling of what would follow over the next generation. The 1950s had unfolded with moderation. The economy returned to a sound postwar footing, while the financial sector remained stable and conservative—thanks in large part to the constraints placed on financial intermediaries during the 1930s. There was a mild business recession in the early 1960s, but nothing of the sort that foreshadowed what was to follow.

We now know that the postwar decades ushered in unprecedented and dramatic changes—akin to the geological tectonic shifts that reshape continents—in financial markets and institutions. The financial environment then is barely recognizable now in both scale and scope. It was a time when financial service firms began to break out of the regulatory

© The Author(s) 2016
H. Kaufman, *Tectonic Shifts in Financial Markets*,
DOI 10.1007/978-3-319-48387-0_1

boundaries within which they had been confined for several decades. Credit and financial institutions stood on the brink of inconceivably explosive growth. Here are just a few examples of changes between 1960 and today:

- In 1960, non-financial debt totaled $1.1 trillion. It is now $6 trillion.
- In 1960, the U.S. government debt totaled $320 billion. It is now $17 trillion.
- In 1960, the mortgage market was not securitized. Today, most mortgages do not remain in the portfolio of their originating institutions, and many ultimately end up in the portfolios of Freddie Mac and Fannie Mae, institutions that had not been in place in 1955.
- In 1960, there were 23,700 insured deposit institutions. There are now only 6,300. Many have merged. In fact, the ten largest financial conglomerates, in which are housed deposit institutions, control more than 75 percent of all American financial assets. As recently as 1990, the ten largest financial firms controlled only 10 percent of total assets.
- In 1960, no one talked about financial derivatives. That market now exceeds $630 trillion.
- In 1960, the net increase of new corporate bond issuance totaled just $3.4 billion. In recent years, quite a few corporations each issued in excess of $5 billion, including $12 billion for Apple, $15 billion for CVS, and $49 billion for Verizon.
- In 1960, the size of the mutual funds industry was $71 billion. Today, its size is $3.6 trillion.

It was also around 1960 that Salomon Brothers began a steep ascent toward becoming a major force in the money and capital markets.

In this book I reflect on some of the tectonic shifts that remade the post-World War II financial world. My approach is impressionistic and often personal, based on my first-hand relationships and encounters with key figures. This is because financial markets and institutions were transformed, not through a broad and deliberate process engineered by political leaders and the banking establishment, but rather through a combination of private action and public inaction. In commercial and investment banking, Walt Wriston, Charlie Sanford, Michael Milken and others pushed new financial strategies and instruments with dramatic—and not always positive—results. For their part, public officials, with few exceptions, failed to consider fully or understand the long-term implications of their measures, however innocuous they seemed at the time. As Sherlock Holmes taught us in "The Hound of the Baskervilles," the dog that doesn't bark can loom as important as the one that does.

For the last six decades, I have been a close observer and participant in the transformative tectonic shifts of our age—by leading the effort to transform research at Salomon Brothers into the world's premier fixed income research organization; by serving in the firm's senior management as a member of the Executive Committee and as vice chairman of the post-partnership holding company (Phibro); and, later, at the helm of my own investment firm and on the board of Lehman Brothers.

***

How I joined Salomon Brothers in the first place—like the larger tableau of postwar financial tectonic shifts—is a story of seemingly minor consequence at the outset but of large import in retrospect. The men who took the gamble to hire someone with my credentials were, in retrospect, visionaries. Not only did I hold a Ph.D. in banking and finance (probably the first person on Wall Street with that degree) but I came out of commercial and central banking; I had not been brought up in investment banking.

Salomon Brothers was founded in 1910. In its first half century in business, the firm earned a reputation in the money and bond markets as being highly competitive. As my doctoral mentor at New York University, Professor Marcus Nadler, observed when I sought his advice about the position: "Henry, at Salomon Brothers, you will soon know whether you will sink or swim—and you will hear the cash register ring every minute of the trading day." As usual, he was correct. My decision to move from the New York Fed to Salomon[1] was influenced most of all by the fact that the firm had hired Sidney Homer, the world's preeminent expert on interest rates. Sidney had devoted his entire career to analyzing and evaluating money and bond markets and was about to publish a seminal book, *A History of Interest Rates*.

Even so, Salomon's decision to hire Sidney in 1961 and me in 1962 was bold and propitious—especially given the fact that no one at Salomon held graduate degrees at the time, and quite a few of the partners didn't even possess an undergraduate degree. These were practical men with street experience, not formal academic training. To hire an analytical wizard such as Sidney, and a Ph.D. in banking and finance was unconventional to say the least. Not even they fully understood at the time the implications of their move. We introduced new analytics that helped turn Salomon into a juggernaut, that eventually were copied by its rivals, and that led to another tectonic shift on Wall Street.

---

[1] My early career in commercial banking and as an economist at the New York Federal Reserve are recounted in Kaufman 2000.

The key proponents behind the decision were Charles Simon, who set up the initial introductions, and William Salomon (better known as Billy), son of one of the firm's founders, who approved the hiring. Charlie had joined the firm as an office boy in 1930, and worked his way up to a senior sales position and eventually to senior partner. Rather than earning degrees, he frequently attended lectures and forums, including sessions of Professor Nadler's seminar "Contemporary Economic and Financial Issues" at NYU's Graduate School of Business Administration. He read widely and deeply, and reveled in sharing his latest insights—and copies of books that inspired him—with colleagues and friends. Charlie also held an abiding interest in American art, and served as Treasurer and Trustee of the Whitney Museum. His knowledge and enthusiasm for American art came to inspire the same in me, which eventually blossomed for me into a satisfying avocation as a collector of American art. Although Charlie's moods swung widely, when it came to the firm's clients, his behavior was steady and fearless. He demanded that every client trade be executed to the highest standards. When that didn't happen, the trader—even if he was a partner—suffered Charlie's rebuke.

Billy Salomon joined the firm in 1933. Only nineteen, he had just graduated from a preparatory school. His father, Percy, was one of the firm's founders. College was the expected next step, but Billy wanted to get married. Percy Salomon believed that married men needed to provide for their families, even if that meant foregoing college, so Billy took a job in the back office. From there he moved to the trading desk, then to sales, and in 1944 he became a partner. When Salomon's financial situation floundered in the latter part of the 1950s, due largely to poor leadership, Billy emerged as the new leader and was designated as the managing partner in 1963.

Billy became the force that moved Salomon Brothers from a money market and bond house to a broadly based investment banking and trading house with national and international recognition. He encouraged the firm to compete aggressively for corporate underwritings, to expand into making markets in equities, and to open offices abroad. He identified talented individuals within the firm, and a few elsewhere, adroitly moving them into key trading, investment banking, and sales positions. He understood that one of the key prerequisites of preserving the growth and stability of the firm was to grow the firm's capital. Accordingly, under Billy's leadership, Salomon held strict limits on partner salaries and on the withdrawal of capital; woe to the partner who approached Billy asking to withdraw above those limits. He also encouraged fierce competition for business, but only to the extent that it did not encroach on the integrity of the firm. In instances when it did—again, whether the perpetrator was a partner or not—Billy's wrath was palpable.

Salomon Brothers asked Sidney Homer to put in place a fixed income research department. No other firms had such an operation. When I joined Salomon Brothers, the research side consisted entirely of Sidney, a research analyst, a statistical clerk, and two secretaries.

One of my first roles at Salomon was to become a "Fed watcher" at a time when very few on Wall Street—perhaps no more than a handful of others—were doing the same. In stark contrast with today, there was precious little data back then. The Fed did not release the deliberations of the FOMC meetings. The Fed chairman held no press conferences. Presidents of the Federal Reserve Banks rarely gave public speeches. Changes in the discount rate and reserve requirements were announced with little fanfare.

I was also charged with analyzing and projecting the flow of funds through the credit markets. This work proved extremely helpful for understanding the workings of the market as well as for long-term forecasts about the direction of interest rates.

In short order, Salomon took a distinctive leadership role in several areas of research: fixed-income, both domestic and international; real estate and mortgage finance; and (less prominently) equities. Maintaining objectivity was always a challenge, but I made it a personal mission to insulate my researchers from pressures coming from the underwriting and trading operations. Salomon's market makers and dealers learned of the firm's major research findings, including my forecasts, from public sources just like the rest of Wall Street. By serving on the highest level of the partnership (the Executive Committee), and later—when the firm was publicly owned—as a member of the Board of Directors and as Vice Chairman, I could effectively shield the research function from undue influence.

One event stands out in my memory. On June 20, 1984, John Reed was reported to have been named to succeed Walter Wriston as Chairman and Chief Executive of Citicorp. The *New York Times* called Tom Hanley, our bank stock analyst, for comment. For many years, Tom had been named the top-ranked bank analyst by the publication *The Institutional Investor*. He was quoted on page one of the newspaper saying, "I can't believe it, I'm shaking. I'm in shock," a comment that immediately reverberated through the financial community.

That same day, coincidentally, Salomon's Executive Committee was scheduled to meet. I anticipated criticism from some of my partners, especially because we had been trying to enlarge both our underwriting and our trading activities with Citi. And, indeed, I was asked what

I intended to "do" about Hanley. I stated categorically that I was not going to ask him to leave, but would talk with him about his demeanor. Along with that, I issued a memo to all of the firm's research analysts. "In speaking to the press," I said, "we should continue to be helpful. Analysts, however, should confine their comments to an elaboration of thoughts generally reflected in written material in their area of responsibility and should not venture forth with views on personalities."

Indeed, one of the key reasons I left Salomon in 1988—along with the fact that the firm was in my view taking on too much risk—was because a firm restructuring reduced my ability to fully safeguard the independence of research. (I was not asked to join the new Office of the Chairman, an internal body that superseded the Executive Committee in power and importance.)

By that time, we were employing about 450 researchers, including both fixed-income and equity analysts, with some 50 holding Ph.D. degrees. I was fortunate to recruit many talented analysts and economists, quite a number of whom went on to build eminent careers. Salomon's bond research operations were widely regarded as the world's best.[2] The 1980s were an astonishingly successful decade for Salomon, which proved beyond doubt the great importance and dynamism of financial markets. In the process, the company became one of the most profitable investment banks in the world.

---

[2] By the 1970s, according to Martin Mayer's account of Salomon's travails after I left the firm, "[Salomon's] monetary and fixed-income (bond) research operations were the best in the world, certainly in the private sector." (Mayer 1993, p. 40)

2

The Art and Science of Forecasting

Today, forecasting is all the rage. A small army of economists and analysts scrutinizes every bit of new information and speedily attempts to predict its implications.

Why is there such a forecasting frenzy today? After all, as Walter Friedman has chronicled in his wry, prize-winning history of economic forecasting, *The Fortune Tellers* (Friedman 2014), some of the most prominent economic minds of the early twentieth century failed to see the Great Depression coming or otherwise blundered massively. Yet the hunger to make educated financial and economic prognostications has endured, in part because the stakes are enormous for investors and householders alike.

In recent decades, financial markets have grown even faster than nominal GDP, while marketable obligations—especially mortgage obligations that for a long time were domiciled with the originating financial institutions—also have mushroomed. The rapid growth of marketable instruments has been buttressed by innovations in trading and by the

© The Author(s) 2016   **9**
H. Kaufman, *Tectonic Shifts in Financial Markets*,
DOI 10.1007/978-3-319-48387-0_2

application of new financial derivatives. Also, computers have vastly improved our ability to collect, store, and evaluate economic and financial data.

With the accelerating growth of financial markets, professional forecasters nevertheless have periodically failed to overcome important behavioral biases. Herding is one of the most troublesome. Most predictions fall within a rather narrow range that does not deviate from consensus views in the financial community. In large measure, this reflects an all-too-human propensity to minimize the risk of failure and to avoid isolation. There is, after all, comfort in running with the crowd. Doing so makes it virtually impossible to be singled out for being wrong, and allows one to avoid the envy or resentment that often inflicts those who are right more often than not. And, as a practical matter, few are ever able to anticipate dramatic shifts in economic and financial behavior. If a large number of market participants were able to do so, acting together they could head off big changes in the first place.

Forecasting is also path dependent—that is, shaped by historical patterns. Whether projections are aimed at the overall performance of an economy or at the individual performance of a firm, they typically rest on an assumption that past cyclical patterns will continue. Statistical averaging—which has become easier and easier with the rise in computational power and with econometrics—tends to reinforce this historical bias. This commonplace tendency to assume that history will repeat itself is understandable, but it carries some notable risks. Economies and financial markets do indeed exhibit some broad, repetitive patterns. Yet as Mark Twain reminds us, while history sometimes rhymes, it does not repeat itself. In fact, the critical ingredient in making good projections often is the ability to understand what *differs* from the past.

The dangers of relying too heavily on historical trends in forecasting became abundantly clear as the post-World War II period unfolded. From the early 1970s through 1981, for instance, interest rates in the United States rose to unprecedented heights that surprised and baffled most observers. Why were so many caught off guard? Because they failed to take into account profound structural changes in the financial markets that ushered in a new period in the credit markets. Until then, moderate increases in interest rates squeezed many would-be debtors out of the market. But in response to the credit crunches of 1966 and 1970, a series of structural shifts—especially the corporate movement toward large contractual lines of credit, the coming of floating-rate financing at banks, and the government's lifting of interest rate ceilings—opened up the credit markets to a greater and greater number of participants. Forecasters who looked to past patterns, but who failed to take full account of recent structural changes, failed to predict the extraordinary interest rate surge of the 1970s.

Another form of bias is widespread and difficult to escape. Simply put, this is the bias against bad news, or negative predictions. In the economic arena we can see this bias at work from financial institutions and business corporations that rarely speak of near-term travails, all the way up to the President's Council of Economic Advisers, the Federal Reserve, and the U.S. Treasury—which seldom if ever predict a pending recession. Across the economic forecasting landscape, positive and neutral news squeezes out negative news.

The bias for positive news springs from many sources. Optimism has served as a key biological mechanism for human survival. And we all know from personal experience that optimism helps us cope with the often-harsh realities of life. Behavioral economists have documented a persistent tendency in people to underestimate risk and the odds of failure. Even though only a tiny percent of new business start-ups in the United States survive more than a few years and those who found businesses make on average less than they would earn working for an established company, each year about 300 out of every 100,000 Americans launch new businesses—some out of opportunity, others out of necessity, all from a sense of optimism (Shane 2008; Fairlie et al. 2015).

Negative forecasts are politically unpopular. In the 1980 presidential contest, Ronald Reagan's optimistic message about the return of American greatness was much more appealing than Jimmy Carter's message about national malaise. In business, corporate leaders—even when they see a poor quarter or profit picture on the horizon—tend not to talk about it. Financial managers who make negative forecasts can suffer from the kill-the-messenger syndrome.

In making forecasts about interest rates and other key indices throughout my career, I have often encountered the fallout that comes to those who make negative predictions. During the tumultuous 1970s, I repeatedly warned of pernicious high inflation rates and the attendant sharp rise in interest rates. I also made unwelcome predictions about the damaging effects of the debt explosion and of the poor supervision of financial institutions. Such admonitions earned me the label "Dr. Doom." Even so, I never wavered from the conviction that accuracy is better than false hope in financial forecasting. The unavoidable reality is that negative predictions may be accurate predictions.

Negative financial forecasts not only pose severe challenges for the forecaster; they are difficult for the business community to act upon. Who really has the capacity to take advantage of news of an impending downturn?

Large corporations and their leaders are constrained by another powerful bias: the growth bias. Few top managers command the power to reverse an expansionary strategy. Shareholders, employees, suppliers and other key stakeholders want to see continued expansion. From top to bottom, business organizations are designed to build market share and to continue an upward trajectory.

The research units in Wall Street firms were hobbled by other biases as well. These biases were especially evident in forecasts involving industries, earnings, economic prospects and interest rates. Then, and still today, the pejorative term for this is "sell-side research." Fortunately, I was always in a position to comment on market developments as I saw them and never took into consideration Salomon's immediate trading or underwriting decisions. My independence was further protected when I became a partner in 1967, and when I later joined Salomon's Executive Committee, I could make sure that objectivity remained a top priority in research. Again, the two men who recruited me in the first place were instrumental in promoting me to the Executive Committee: Charlie Simon, who proposed the appointment, and Billy Salomon, who approved it. They understood that objective research would benefit the long-term interest of the firm and add to its integrity. As far as I know, no other Wall Street firm promoted its head of research to the highest level of senior management.

As for *long-term* forecasting, there is simply no scientific methodology that can produce accurate predictions. As much as we crave long-term predictions, and forecasting gurus make such claims, the goal is beyond the reach of their techniques. With that said, here are a few lessons I took away from that long phase of my career.

First, history shows that to project the future by merely extending the past is a dangerous thing. I spoke about this in the more narrow sense of relying on past data to model the future. Here I am speaking about the major geopolitical events that reshape economies and nations. A look back at the previous century underscores the point. The decade of the 1910s was marked by World War I; the 1920s by speculation; the 1930s by worldwide depression; the 1940s by global war; the 1950s by economic recovery and rehabilitation; the 1960s by a long economic expansion that sowed the seeds of inflation; the 1970s by oil shortages and unprecedented stagflation; the 1980s by disinflation and deregulation; and the 1990s by global securitization and financial speculation that led to crisis early in this century.

Second, leadership—whether in business, finance, industry, or culture—follows a life cycle. The duration of this life cycle varies. We need only look to the Roman Empire, ancient Greece, and Spain for examples of *former* empires. In the business world, IBM was unknown when American railroads occupied the premier position in financial markets. Who really anticipated the impact of Microsoft, Apple, or Google?

Third, beware of economic fashions. They contribute to unsustainable business momentum, either up or down. For some time, the fashion in economics has been elaborate modeling that (as I've noted) relies too heavily on historical data. Technique has taken precedence over wide-ranging analysis.

Consider how hard it would have been, from the vantage point of 1945, to predict most of the world's major transformations since then. Standing in the ruins of total war, did Western Europe's spectacular rise seem plausible? Or Japan's? And as those unfolded, did the emergence of the BRICs seem likely? Multinational corporations had been around for a century, but who anticipated their rapid spread after the Second World War, along with the meteoric rise of international financial networks?

Imbedded in forecasting dilemmas are some deeper uncertainties—namely periodic tectonic shifts in the financial markets (which I discuss in greater detail later) caused by market events and official responses that alter the structure of the financial markets and, in many ways, have unintended consequences. This, I believe, is evident when the post-World War II era is examined not from a cyclical but from a broader perspective. The first period spans from the early 1950s to 1962, years in which the economy moved away from war footings but lived with the financial regulations imposed in the 1930s. Next was the period from 1962 to 2008, when financial freedom reigned eventually, and this too has had its unintended consequences. A new period started in 2008 against a backdrop of financial failures and new official financial legislation. There is now a longing to return to some phase of financial and monetary normality, whatever that may be. However, we cannot put humpty-dumpty back together again. The unintended consequences of the period that ended in 2008 are still unfolding and the financial landscape is in the process of being materially altered.

3

Presidents versus Fed Chairmen

Just as the political system in the United States is based on the separation of powers, our federal economic bureaucracy possesses some components under direct executive control, and others that are supposed to operate independently. Among the latter, none is more prominent than the Federal Reserve System. The Fed is officially charged with maintaining stable economic growth through monetary policy. This is a goal any president should embrace, yet since its founding in 1913 the Fed often has found itself at odds with one or another presidential administration.

Many of the conflicts have been rooted in the tension between long-term and shorter-term economic goals; the Fed is supposed to favor the latter, whereas the reality of electoral politics makes presidents much more sensitive to the near horizon. Yet even when standing up to political pressure, the Fed often has fallen short of meeting its goals because of various forms of myopia.

© The Author(s) 2016
H. Kaufman, *Tectonic Shifts in Financial Markets*,
DOI 10.1007/978-3-319-48387-0_3

17

During the 1960s and 1970s, the Federal Reserve often did a poor job of controlling inflation. In large measure, this failure was due to central bankers' inability to understand how the relaxation of financial regulations would affect the workings of monetary policy. When the Fed began to lift the ceilings on bank deposits in the early 1960s, for example, few foresaw the consequences of easing Regulation Q, a step that allowed banks to become bidders for funds in the open credit market. This short-coming in Fed policy became even more significant as financial markets were further deregulated in the 1980s and 1990s. The Fed had to raise interest rates to higher levels than before (under the same conditions) in order to slow inflation. As the deregulated private sector invented and mass produced new credit instruments (such as off-balance-sheet deriva-tives of various sorts), the Fed found itself in a weaker and weaker posi-tion for controlling the rapid creation of credit.

During and for a while after the Second World War, the Federal Reserve supported federal borrowing by holding the interest rate on US Treasury bills at 0.375 percent and the long government bond at 2.5 percent. But in 1951, William McChesney Martin, then head of the Import–Export Bank, was called to Washington to mediate negotiations over what became known as the 1951 Accord (or Fed-Treasury Accord). Six days after the Accord was released, Fed Chairman Thomas B. McCabe stepped down. President Truman appointed fellow Democrat Martin, hoping to bring the Fed into line. But the new chairman had other ideas, exercising new authority under the Accord and concentrating policymaking power through the Federal Open Market Committee.

When President Truman and Bill Martin crossed each other's paths quite coincidentally at the Waldorf-Astoria in late 1951, the Fed Chairman said "Good afternoon, Mr. President." The President looked

Martin in the eye and replied with a single word: "Traitor." Martin also was assailed by President Lyndon Johnson. On December 2, 1965, Martin's Fed raised interest rates for the first time in five years. Johnson had explicitly opposed the move, fearful the rate hike could dampen economic prosperity and endanger the Great Society and the Vietnam War. He summoned Bill Martin to his ranch in Johnson City, Texas, for what the president called a "trip to the woodshed." Johnson berated Martin for taking an action the president disapproved that "can affect my entire term." But Martin stood firm, which burnished the central bank's reputation for independence (Bremner 2004, pp. 1–2).

The most amusing confrontation with President Johnson was actually told to me by Bill Martin after he had retired from the Fed. He had been called with great urgency to come over to the White House to meet with the president. The chairman rushed over rather fearfully, not knowing what to expect. The president saw him in the Oval Office. He then told Martin to hold in great confidence what he was about to say. With that the President stood up, dropped his pants and said, roughly, "Now Bill I am going to have an operation around here (pointing to the lower part of his body), and you aren't going to raise interest rates while I am temporarily incapacitated, are you?"

When Bill Martin became chairman of the Fed, he had served as chairman of the New York Stock Exchange, head of the Export–Import Bank, and assistant secretary for monetary affairs at the U.S. Treasury. In the 1960s, he became quite uncomfortable with the changing financial and economic scene. In 1965, in a commencement speech at Columbia University, he warned of "disquieting similarities" between the late 1920s, before the Great Crash, and the 1960s boom then in its seventh year. "Our common goals of maximum employment, production, and purchasing power can be realized only if we are willing to prevent orderly expansion from turning into disorderly boom" ("Martin Compares...," *New York Times*, June 2, 1965). Martin also reminded his audience that in the 1920s many experts claimed that "a new economic era had opened." He was referring to the belief that the economy was expanding without interruption. Martin was correct on that point: business cycles are endemic to capitalism. But he did not fully appreciate through his Fed chairmanship that the forces of restraint in place during his early career were being overtaken by structural changes in the markets and by new kinds of financial entrepreneurialism. Even so, Bill Martin was a formidable leader during a critical formative stage in the modern Federal Reserve System, and he fought hard to protect the Fed's quasi independence.

His successor at the Fed, Arthur Burns, also brought excellent credentials to his chairmanship (1970–1978). He was a business cycle expert, a former Chairman of the Council of Economic Advisers, and a distinguished professor at Columbia University. In person, Burns projected gravitas and erudition, enhanced by his pipe smoking and the careful attention he seemed to be paying to what you were telling him. Although his voice was rather high-pitched, he spoke in a slow, measured cadence that conveyed a sense of wisdom and thoughtfulness. In the numerous meetings I had with him, I was always impressed by these attributes; and I suspect so were many others.

Burns was appointed by President Nixon, who blamed part of his failed bid for the White House in 1960 on stringent Fed policy and saw Burns as more pliable than Martin. By and large, he was right. The two men had a tense relationship, with Burns typically giving in. Burns allowed Nixon's staff to vet his speeches, and publicly pledged to remain the president's "true friend" on economic policies. He opposed only tepidly Nixon's closing of the gold window, as well as the Administration's wage and price controls. Inflation doubled from 6 to 12 percent under Burns mainly because he succumbed to Nixonian pressure for expansionary monetary policy. His reputation damaged by double-digit inflation, Burns actually instructed the Fed's staff to come up with measures that would exclude food and energy from the consumer price index.

Burns devoted much of his Per Jacobsson Lecture in Belgrade (where the International Monetary Fund met in 1979) trying to justify, in retrospect, the U.S. central bank's record on inflation under his chairmanship. Revealingly, the talk was titled "The Anguish of Central Banking." Congress had been working hard to create jobs, Burns asserted, leaving his Fed little room to maneuver. "The persistent inflation that plagues the industrial democracies will not be vanquished—or even substantially curbed—until new currents of thought create a political environment in which difficult adjustments required to end inflation can be undertaken" (Burns 1979). Like Burns' actions in 1970s, his words reflected lack of vision or forceful leadership. And he had never fully understood the linkages between financial markets and the business sector.

Tensions between Fed chairmen and their presidents persist to the present day, although Executive Branch pressure has become more subtle and less direct. It is hard to imagine a present-day "trip to the woodshed." Perhaps presidential preferences are conveyed through operatives; certainly, they are no longer public. Another reason presidents no longer visibly lean on Fed chairmen is because the latter have become relatively more powerful as monetary policy itself has gained in prominence since the late 1970s.

Following Arthur Burns, G. William Miller served as Fed chairman for a short (seventeen-month) stint beginning March 1978. Miller had spent most of his career in corporate America (at Textron), and was far from an inflation hawk. His resistance to raising interest rates in the face of high inflation pummeled the value of the dollar, leading the Carter Administration to launch a "dollar rescue package," and other Fed Governors to overrule Miller in 1979 by voting to raise the discount rate. Oddly, President Carter appointed Miller as U.S. treasury secretary after his poor leadership at the Fed. I discuss his successor, Paul Volcker, in the next chapter, and Volcker's successors, Alan Greenspan, Ben Bernanke, and Janet Yellen, in the one after that.

Many postwar Fed chairmen have served across party lines—a good sign. Unlike Supreme Court justices, they are not appointed for life. We need guardians of our economy and financial system with consistent, long-term vision. But events in the last few decades suggest that the Federal Reserve is well on the way to being heavily politicized—a problem I reflect on in a later chapter.

4

Paul Volcker, Perennial Public Servant

Very soon after I joined the Federal Reserve Bank of New York as an economist in 1957, I encountered a very tall man. I was walking down the ninth-floor corridor of the Research Department. Coming toward me was a man chewing on a cigar, about six and a half feet tall, deeply engrossed in writing notes on a yellow pad as he walked. I greeted him and said, "I am Henry Kaufman." "Well," he responded, "I'm Paul Volcker. You're the new fellow in Financial and Trade" (a division of the Research Department). With a "good luck" sort of "good bye," he rambled on.

By the time I joined the New York Fed, Paul already had been there five years and was steeply ascending the learning curve. He had helped Robert V. Roosa, the head of Research, draft *Federal Reserve Operations in the Money and Government Securities Markets* (1956), a valuable guide to Fed operations with a distinctive red cover. By the time I joined Salomon Brothers in 1962, I had, like many on Wall Street, virtually committed

© The Author(s) 2016
H. Kaufman, *Tectonic Shifts in Financial Markets*,
DOI 10.1007/978-3-319-48387-0_4

much of this publication to memory. Paul and I both spent time at the New York Fed's open market desk, where it traded securities, although his stint there lasted much longer than my three weeks. So when I arrived at the Fed's Research Department (after working on credit at an industrial bank, then at a New York commercial bank, for about eight years), Paul Volcker was among the unit's senior economists. I suspect Bob Roosa took me on at the New York Fed because of my banking experience, a strong recommendation from my academic mentor, Professor Marcus Nadler, and the fact that I was just one year away from completing a doctorate degree at New York University.

I saw little of Paul during my early months at the Fed. He left later in 1957 to join the Chase Manhattan Bank as an economist. But I reconnected with Paul, and saw him regularly for a number of years, thanks to "the Foursome." This was the brainchild of Al Wojnilower, who had left the New York Fed for First National City Bank, then became the economist for The First Boston Corporation, a very prominent investment bank at the time. Al suggested that he, Volcker, I, and Leonard Santow—then at Aubrey G. Lanston, a highly regarded U.S. government bond dealer—meet periodically for lunch to talk about economics and finance. As Paul reflected in an interview, "In the 1960s Wojnilower, Kaufman, Leonard Santow from the Dallas Fed in Texas and I began to have regular exchanges of opinion, calling our group, the 'Foursome.'" Paul left the luncheon group in 1973, when he moved to the U.S. Treasury. Others, including Dennis Weatherstone, the CEO of Morgan Guaranty, and Charles Sanford, the CEO of the Bankers Trust, rotated in.

Paul and I kept in touch through phone conversations, occasional lunches, dinners with our wives, and my visits to his offices in New York and in Washington. After he became a private citizen in 1987, Paul organized an annual birthday get-together called "The Class of 1927" for several of us, like Paul and me, born that year. The celebration also included Sam Cross (formerly an executive vice president of the New York Fed), Richard Gardner (formerly an ambassador to Italy and Spain), Shijuro Ogata (formerly deputy governor of the Bank of Japan) and his wife, Sadako (formerly United Nations high commissioner for refugees), and Happy Rockefeller (wife of Governor Nelson Rockefeller). These dinners, which each of us hosted at various times in our homes, brimmed with nostalgia and camaraderie.

With this introduction about my relationship with Paul in mind, I am obviously not the most objective commentator on Paul. Still, let me offer some observations about his life and career that I believe I can state dispassionately.

Paul was not to the manor born. He was raised in the middle-class northern New Jersey town of Teaneck, where his father, trained as a civil engineer, served as town manager for two decades. Paul A. Volcker, Sr., helped navigate Teaneck through the Great Depression and was known as unwaveringly fair and deliberative. His devotion to public service as a high calling no doubt influenced his son.

Following Paul's chairmanship of the U.S. Federal Reserve from 1979 to 1987, he has remained extremely active in public life, apart from serving as chairman of Wolfensohn & Co., a New York investment bank. Along with many other public posts, he has headed a commission to investigate the accounts of holocaust victims in Swiss accounts; worked for the United Nations investigating the Iraqi Oil for Food program; chaired the Washington-based Group of Thirty; and headed President Obama's Economic Recovery Advisory Board. He currently heads the Volcker Alliance, a non-partisan group of business, academic, and government interests devoted to "effective execution of public policies and [helping] rebuild public trust in government," according to its mission statement. Paul seems to relish these involvements in spite of their often considerable frustrations. I suspect he has never been completely comfortable in the private sector.

Paul writes extremely well. He edits to the point of fault. Sometimes, he'll relinquish a speech or paper only because of a looming deadline. He tailors his style to the genre, whether a book, speech, position paper, or internal memorandum. He has become deft at lacing his remarks with bits of humor. Even now, in his ninetieth year, his recall of events, some decades old, is quite remarkable.

Another trait that has served Paul quite well is that he keeps his own counsel. He will rarely initiate a conversation, but prefers to observe a discussion unfold, taking its measure, and then responding. He is a skillful observer and listener. And when he does comment, his observations are careful and on point; rarely will he delve into matter of personality unless among those he trusts a great deal. Paul is also known for his deliberateness and persistence. I witnessed these traits when I accompanied him on some fly fishing expeditions—a sport that demands extraordinary patience, precision, and even artistry.

When President Carter asked Paul Volcker to become Fed chairman, the U.S. economy was in disarray, which I will discuss in a moment. Privately, Paul also faced grave challenges as he pondered the decision. The move would mean a deep pay cut from the $110,000 salary he was earning as president of the New York Fed to the $57,000 Fed chairman's salary. His wife, Barbara, was suffering from debilitating arthritis and diabetes, and his son, Jimmy, had cerebral palsy. After he accepted the position, Paul lived very frugally in Washington during the week, while his family remained in New York. He never complained about it, and few were fully aware of this hardship.

Along with his deep commitment to public service, Paul recognized that the offer of a Fed chairmanship doesn't come along often. Because Jimmy Carter's presidency was struggling, it was likely he would be succeeded by a Republican. Volcker and other Democrats therefore might have to wait four or eight more years, perhaps even longer, for another opportunity to head the central bank.

Yet the challenges facing the new Fed chairman were staggering and unprecedented. As I discussed in "The Presidents v. the Fed Chairmen," the record of central bankers in the post-World War II period had been mixed at best. Arthur Burns had been a poor guardian of the Fed's independence, and President Carter was looking to replace G. William Miller, who ultimately served only fourteen months. The U.S. economy began to suffer from high inflation in the mid-1960s, when the Johnson administration continued to scale up both the Great Society and the Vietnam War at a time when the economy was running at near capacity, and refused for years to raise taxes. Macroeconomic conditions worsened considerably in the mid-1970s, when President Nixon closed the gold window and oil embargos plagued the global economy. The U.S. inflation rate hit double digits and economic growth slowed to a crawl—the dire combination dubbed "stagflation." Out of desperation, the conservative Republican president instituted wage and price controls, a merely temporary palliative. His Democratic successor, President Jimmy Carter, also acting out of character, instituted a wave of deregulation (widely associated with President Reagan) in an effort to jump-start the economy.

As the chief monetary authority, the Fed was not officially charged with sustaining economic growth (even though recent Fed chairmen apparently have seen that as one of their responsibilities). Inflation was another matter. Seemingly immune to Fed measures for some fifteen years, it was now soaring to unprecedented levels. As inflation always does, it discouraged savings, hurt those on fixed incomes, and eroded confidence in the future. By most accounts it was the number one economic policy problem facing the nation.

In his interview with President Carter, before the president announced Paul's nomination, he had told the President that interest rates would have to be raised. However, if the president had known what Paul was going to do, I doubt that he would have nominated him. Imagine how aghast the president would have been if Paul had been required to provide forward guidance, including a three-year economic and financial forecast of the type the Fed now provides. Politically, Paul's remedies would have been unacceptable to the president and his close advisors. The economic and financial situation that confronted the new chairman in the fall of 1979 was stark. Paul, of course, was aware of these disturbing developments. As president of the New York Fed, he had been serving as vice chairman of the Federal Open Market Committee.

Within two months, he had convinced the FOMC to reorient, and soon the Fed announced that it would pursue a monetarist policy approach. It would supply a steady but only moderate volume of new reserves to the market, while disregarding their interest rate implications. Yet the Fed gave no assurances of a permanent commitment to this approach as a kind of new golden rule of monetary policy. The pressing goal was to wring inflation out of the economy. Paul Volcker had become monetarist for the time being.

Immediately following the announcements of the Fed's new stance, financial markets reacted dramatically. Some dubbed the central bank's actions a "Saturday Night Massacre." The Fed's actions generated great pressure in the money market, where rates shot up 60 to 150 basis points in the US, and by as much as 160 basis points in the Euro CD market. At Salomon Brothers, we felt the repercussions of the Fed's decisions immediately. We had been awarded the lead position for a $1 billion underwriting for IBM—the first public bond issuance by the corporation. It was a coup for Salomon. We replaced Morgan Stanley as IBM's banker. We priced the issue very aggressively on Friday, the day before Paul's announcements. By the end of the next week, the bonds were selling at a five-point discount. Although we had covered part of our risk by shorting some holdings, we suffered a significant loss. Still, we didn't regret our aggressiveness, because it enhanced our relationship with IBM and helped boost us to the top ranks of corporate investment bankers.

I expressed my views about the Fed's landmark decision in our weekly *Comments on Credit* published on Friday following the Fed's announcement (Fig. 4.1).

I explained that the Fed's abandonment of a federal funds target in favor of a reserve growth target would, for the first time in many years, discourage investors from credit market arbitrage. For too long, I pointed out, Fed laxity—because of its failure to understand structural change in financial markets—had essentially removed money risk from institutional lending. Now, the gap between interest rates and the inflation rate was closing fast.

Within the Fed, too, Paul opted to do the right thing as he saw it rather than striving to win a popularity contest akin to what Alan Greenspan did while he was Fed chair. In order to push through his anti-inflation policies, Paul had to overcome contrary views within the Board of Governors. The initial vote to raise the discount rate passed by a mere four to three.

Salomon Brothers

Members of the New York Stock Exchange, Inc.

One New York Plaza
New York, N.Y. 10004

Comments on Credit

October 12, 1979

A Landmark Monetary Decision. Last weekend, the Federal Reserve announced a series of credit restraining decisions that quickly reverberated through all sectors of the credit markets. The increase in the discount rate by 1% was a traditional move. The imposition of marginal reserve requirements on managed bank liabilities had some unusual features. But the abandonment of a narrow Federal funds rate target in favor of a reserve growth target is a decisive and extraordinary monetary decision.

The total ramifications will still have to filter through the economy and the credit markets. Initially, the announcement of the decision put substantial price pressures on all sectors of the financial markets. In the few days following the announcement, the price give-ups in the fixed income area were unprecedented. Interest rates, which had been moving just through the cyclical peaks reached in 1974-75, are now all at new secular highs with the exception of the tax-exempt market. In addition, yield spread relationships in key sectors of the market, particularly quality spreads, have started to widen significantly (see story below)

The Fed's decisive action came against a backdrop of mounting inflation, rapid credit extensions, and excessive monetary creation, reflecting to a large extent the central bank's inability or unwillingness to deal with the inflationary problem with the established monetary techniques. The Federal Reserve, for a long time, either failed to recognize or neglected the changing structure in our financial institutions. The Fed's neglect increasingly gave institutional lenders the opportunity to take the money risk out of lending. More and more, institutions were able to successfully arbitrage the rates of return on financial assets against the cost of liabilities. As a result, interest rate levels themselves were not the powerful regulator of economic activity that they once were. The crucial factor was the interest rate spread between the cost of liabilities to financial institutions and the yield on their assets.

The Fed's landmark decision has quickly narrowed the gap between the rate of inflation and interest rates. The decision to eliminate a narrow Federal funds rate target has introduced a substantial element of uncertainty, that should slow

Fig. 4.1   Comments on Credit, October 12, 1979

arbitraging in the credit markets. No longer can institutional lenders rely on that benchmark in estimating the spread relationships between the cost of their liabilities and rate of return on their assets.

Although it will take some time before the full consequences of this new monetary policy approach manifest themselves, some developments should become evident in the weeks ahead.

- The rate of commercial bank credit growth should slow; although, in the near term, demand for bank loans will probably continue to be strong. This demand, however, will at least partly have to be met by banks through the liquidation of their securities holdings (see story below). This will contribute to additional pressures in the U.S. Government market and particularly in the municipal market, where commercial banks play a substantial investing and underwriting role.

- The money market operations of commercial banks will become a very important benchmark. The negotiable CD and bank paper rates will take on added importance (perhaps replacing the now highly volatile funds rate) because they will reflect the market judgment of bank issuers, who now must contend with greater risks as well as huge and possibly erratic loan demand in the near term.

- Mutual savings banks will be less able to offset the higher costs of their deposit liabilities, therefore squeezing their declining net operating income even more. Savings and loan associations, many of which have substantial mortgage commitments to meet, will find it more difficult to issue profitably mortgage-backed bonds and pass-through obligations. One likely result will be a larger volume of borrowings from the Federal Home Loan Bank to cover financing demands; another will be a slowdown in new mortgage commitments.

- The volume of new corporate bond issues is likely to abate for a short period, while new trading ranges are established and corporate treasurers reassess their financing strategies. In the short run, the demand for short-term financing will accelerate and then be followed by a very large volume of new bond offerings.

- In the secondary market, the trading matrices, that guided portfolio managers during the past few years, will no longer be appropriate. Interest rates are moving farther into unchartered grounds. Inter and intra-market yield relationships are widening, while larger differentials between bid and asked quotes in secondary market transactions are inevitable.

Fig. 4.1 (continued)

The market viewed this split vote with apprehension, and some questioned the new chairman's leadership abilities. Nor did Paul have an easy time of persuading the FOMC to accept the move to monetarism. In 1986, he was initially also outvoted four to three in two decisions to lower the discount rate by board members who had been placed on the Board by President Reagan. The Board reversed its decision later that day after Paul threatened to resign.

Meanwhile, prominent members of the academic community were highly critical of Paul, especially Milton Friedman, the leading proponent of monetarism, who was also quite influential in Washington and even proposed, provocatively, to disband the Fed altogether. (Friedman believed that strict monetary expansion and reserve expansion, period, was the right formula.) In the business and financial community, Paul's chief adversary probably was Walter Wriston, the head of Citibank (whom I discuss in the next chapter). Even though Wriston initially supported Volcker's appointment as Fed chairman, the two men came to clash on a variety of fronts—from branch banking, to the expansion of banks into activities beyond traditional banking, to reserve requirements, to how to best resolve Latin American debt problems. "Where I come apart with [Volcker] is I believe in markets ..." Wriston told a reporter in 1982. "I believe in deregulation and I think it's fair to say that Paul did not." When asked what he thought of Volcker, Wriston replied "I'll answer that if you tell me what you think of your editor" (Zweig 1995, p. 676).

For its part, organized labor hardly extolled Paul's leadership publicly. I witnessed union anti-Volcker disdain first-hand during one of my visits to Paul's office in Washington. When I asked his secretary why building bricks were piled up in the office, she replied that the bricklayers' union had left them with a note explaining that "we don't need them anymore." The implication was clear: the bricklayers held Volcker responsible for the contraction in new housing construction.

I should note that along with all the criticism Paul confronted as he enacted the tough measures to bring inflation under control, he also benefitted from a general sense among the public that the time had come for serious action. Other Fed and presidential actions (such as wage and price controls) simply hadn't worked. But this in no way detracts from Paul's leadership, for previous Fed chairmen had lacked both a full understanding of what needed to be done and the will to do it.

I have supported many of Paul's economic and financial views and many of his actions, and admire him enormously. Even friends differ sometimes. Here are a few examples of where my views have diverged from Paul's. To begin with, he supported the passage of the Dodd-Frank legislation, whereas I did not. (I explain my deep reservations about Dodd Frank in a later chapter.) Second, I favor the creation of a commission to review and recommend changes in the structure of the Federal Reserve (which I also detail in a later chapter), whereas Paul does not favor central bank restructuring. I suspect he believes—in the spirit of the proverb "the devil you know is better than the one you don't"—that there are more pressing issues at the Fed.

This is a practical streak of his: to work within the system. A couple of years ago, Paul reflected back on inquiries into monetary, credit, and fiscal policies conducted by the Senate (by the Joint Economic Committee chaired by Senator Paul Douglas) beginning in 1949, and by the private Commission on Money and Credit (chaired by Frazer B. Wilde) about a decade later. Noting that these investigations did not lead to consolidation or other restructuring of the regulatory agencies, Volcker observed that nevertheless "something crucially important was achieved." The investigators "reinforced the rationale for Fed independence," insured "adequate resources," and supported "a growing role for active counter-cyclical fiscal policy." The "extreme" views of populists and liberals, Volcker was pleased to note, had been rejected (Volcker 2013).

The Volcker Rule, which prohibits high-risk speculation by the bank, is another example of Paul's proclivity to push for attainable goals. The Rule supposedly pushes banking back to its more conventional activities in the past, and thus enhances the strength of the payments, one of the essential prerequisites for a well-functioning financial system. But in devoting so much effort to the passage of the Volcker Rule, the Fed did not give enough attention to the overriding financial issue, namely the very high concentration of financial assets controlled by a few financial institutions. Financial concentration is seriously undermining the Fed's ability to act freely and effectively. (That topic, too, I discuss in a later chapter.) From my perspective, Paul has not confronted this serious issue head-on.

It is difficult today to fully comprehend the enormity of the task that Volcker confronted when he became chairman in 1979. Figure 4.2 offers an overview of some major economic and financial indicators for the

	Real GDP	Unemployment Rate	Change in Consumer Price Index	3-Month U.S. Bill Rate	Long U.S. Govt. Bond Yield	S&P 500 Stock Index
1979	3.2%	5.8%	13.3%	10.0%	9.3%	108
1980	-0.2	7.1	12.5	11.5	11.3	136
1981	2.8	7.6	8.9	14.0	13.5	123
1982	-1.9	9.7	3.8	10.7	12.8	141
1983	4.8	9.6	3.8	8.6	11.2	165
1984	7.3	7.5	3.9	9.5	12.4	167
1985	4.2	7.2	3.8	7.5	10.8	211
1986	3.5	7.0	1.1	6.0	7.8	242
1987	3.5	6.2	4.4	5.8	8.6	247

Fig. 4.2 Key economic measures during the Volcker Fed chairmanship
Source: Economic Report of the President, Washington, D.C,. February 2015
Note: Data reflects annual averages Peak yields in 1980-81 were as follows: Prime loan rate was 21 1/2% and yields were 17 1/4% for 3-month U.S. Treasury bills and 15 1/4% for long U.S. Government bonds.

years of Volcker's chairmanship. The Volcker Fed's initial move to tighten credit quite evidently was not enough. These data in fact understate the task that Volcker confronted because—at their peak—consumer prices in the running at an annual rate of 15 percent in the first quarter of 1980, 3-month Treasury bills had reached 17.25 percent in 1981, and long government bond yields soared as high as 15 percent during the early 1980s.

But with considerable tenacity, Volcker persevered with the policies that eventually worked over his eight-year term. Consumer prices fell from 13.3 percent in 1979 to 4.4 percent in 1987. After an initial decline, real GDP growth steadied out to a 3–5 percent range. Interest rates, initially pushed much higher by the tight credit policy, ultimately fell from 10 percent in 1979 for the 3-month Treasury bill to 5.8 percent in 1987, while the S&P 500 Stock Index climbed from 108 to 247 during the same period.

Paul Volcker succeeded in dealing with what was probably the most serious economic challenge to confront the U.S. since the Second World War. If our nation had continued to endure dangerously high levels of inflation, our national strength and global leadership would have been compromised. Only within the last few decades has Paul received the recognition he deserves—as a living treasure and an American icon.

5

The Fed and Financial Markets: Greenspan, Bernanke, and Yellen

In recent decades, three Fed chairs have garnered more attention than arguably any previous central bankers in U.S. history.[1] Alan Greenspan became the second-longest serving Fed chairman after heading the bank from 1987 to 2006. He presided over a period of economic expansion, but became controversial in his final term and beyond, after the financial crisis hit in 2007. His successor, Benjamin Bernanke was by necessity a central figure by virtue of grappling with the crisis. Both men were appointed by Republican presidents, inflation hawks, neoliberal monetarists willing to infuse massive amounts of liquidity into the system during times of emergency, and unlikely celebrities. And both Greenspan and Bernanke, for all their accomplishments, remained rather tone deaf

---

[1] Two very visible and controversial central bankers—though neither chaired the Fed—were Nicholas Biddle, who served as the third and last president of the Second Bank of the United States from 1823 to 1836, during the famous "bank war" with President Andrew Jackson over Bank's recharter (it was a central bank in only some respects); and Benjamin Strong, Jr., the first head of the Federal Reserve Bank of New York from 1914 to 1928, when that branch was by far the most powerful in the system.

© The Author(s) 2016
H. Kaufman, *Tectonic Shifts in Financial Markets*,
DOI 10.1007/978-3-319-48387-0_5

to structural changes in financial markets and how those affected monetary policy. Now the spotlight is on Fed chairwoman Janet Yellen. Thus far she has fallen prey to the same hazard.

From Wall Street to Main Street, Alan Greenspan already possessed somewhat of a public persona when he became Paul Volcker's successor at the helm of the Federal Reserve in the summer of 1987, though nothing like the celebrity status he would later command. Quite knowledgeable about business economics, Greenspan nevertheless was not an expert on monetary policy. Unlike Volcker, he spent most of his career in private consulting. His only stints in public service were as Chairman of the Council of Economic Advisers under President Ford (1974–1977), and as chair of the bipartisan National Commission on Social Security Reform under President Reagan. Even so, Greenspan was a loyal Republican and was well-connected politically by the mid-1980s, when President Reagan decided not to reappoint Volcker to the Fed.

Greenspan's honeymoon was brief. First he had to tighten monetary policy, and that was followed in short order by a stock market crash in October 1987. (On the worst day, October 19, the Dow fell nearly 23 percent.) Greenspan's Fed injected massive liquidity into the system, averting broad damage to financial markets and the economy and burnishing the new central banker's reputation.

For several years, the Greenspan Fed eased credit conditions, which helped bolster significant economic expansion in the early 1990s, but was accompanied by extremely rapid credit expansion. When the bank's easing posture ended in 1993, debt continued to pile up. The derivatives market was exploding, but Greenspan repeatedly resisted efforts to regulate the instruments—out of his convictions that the market would self-regulate and that securitization was distributing (and therefore diffusing) risk internationally. Meanwhile, as stock and home prices surged, it was clear that the broader economy was buoyed by the "wealth effect," and Greenspan was loath to risk killing the boom by taking away the proverbial punch bowl. The Fed adjusted the funds rate only modestly throughout the decade.

On the surface, it seemed an almost heroic period for the Federal Reserve. However, Greenspan failed to address critical structural changes, especially the expansion of debt at a much faster rate than GDP, and the rapid growth of marketable securities, including financial derivatives. The precipitous growth of the latter, in turn, facilitated rapid increases in off-balance-sheet transactions at financial institutions. Greenspan held firm to his belief that these obligations served to spread risk-taking and therefore reduce risk for individual investors. And he remained convinced that market operations would automatically rein in excessive risk-taking.

Financial markets concluded otherwise. The stock market proved to be extremely volatile during Greenspan's tenure, climbing steeply in the 1990s and early 2000s, with a major correction in the so-called dot.com sector in 2000, and in 2008, after he had left the Fed. It turned out that markets did not automatically discipline excessive risk-taking, a fact that Greenspan admitted while testifying before Congress in October 2008 about the ongoing financial crisis. "I found a flaw," he admitted, "in the model that I perceived is the critical functioning structure that defines how the world works, so to speak." Representative Henry Waxman followed up: "In other words, you found that your view of the world, your ideology, was not right, it was not working." To which Greenspan replied: "Precisely. That's precisely the reason I was shocked, because I had been going for forty years or more with very considerable evidence that it was working exceptionally well" (U.S. House of Representatives 2008).

Greenspan's Fed not only exercised little restraint on the up side, it provided a floor for investors in the form of what became known as the "Greenspan put." Like a put option, which gives an asset holder the right to sell to a counterparty at a particular price, Greenspan's Fed typically would cut rates following significant market corrections. This injected a great deal of moral hazard into the markets.

A centerpiece of Greenspan's efforts to liberalize markets was his role in the ultimate demise of the Glass-Steagall Act. This came about in a remarkable way—through the joint efforts of the Republican Fed chairman working in concert with two leading Democrats, U.S. Treasury Secretary Robert Rubin and his deputy secretary, Larry Summers. The Gramm-Leach-Bliley Act of 1999—also supported by President Clinton—removed the barrier between commercial and investment banking and other key provisions of Glass-Steagall that had survived more than six decades. In taking this step, none of the powerful economic policymakers demonstrated that they had thought deeply about the consequences of such deregulation for the structure of financial institutions—especially how it opened the door for financial concentration on an unprecedented scale. As I discuss later in this book (Chaps. 7 and 12), extreme financial concentration has damaged not only the operation of financial markets, but also the ability of the Federal Reserve to influence their operation for the better.

Alan Greenspan therefore left his biggest imprint more through what he failed to do—rein in credit and investment bubbles, regulate derivatives, control financial concentration, and later (under President George W. Bush) speak out against burgeoning deficits—than what he did. This is ironic because Greenspan transformed the office of the Fed chairman into a position of some celebrity. Fed watchers, big-time Wall Street players, and ordinary investors alike pored over his famously convoluted utterances—not because they feared a firm hand of control, but because trillions of dollars of additional assets had become marketable during his tenure, and Fed actions influenced the pricing of those assets.

His successor—Princeton economics professor Benjamin Bernanke—had been appointed to the Board of Governors by President Bush, where he served from 2002 to 2005. He then served two years as head of the Council of Economic Advisers, and became chairman of the Federal Reserve on February 1, 2006. In spite of these public appointments, Mr. Bernanke was not as politically connected as Greenspan had been when he took office. Bernanke had built much of his academic reputation on his analysis of the Great Depression, so his appointment seemed propitious in 2008, at the onset of the greatest financial calamity in U.S. and global history since the 1930s. Those who quickly consulted his 2000 book *Essays on the Great Depression* found strong clues as to how he would steer monetary policy during the crisis. "I believe there is now overwhelming evidence that the main factor depressing aggregate demand was a world-wide contraction in world money supplies"[2] (Bernanke 2000, p. viii). Indeed, Bernanke already had garnered the moniker "Helicopter Ben" for quoting Milton Friedman's observation that the best way to address deflation was to drop (that is, print) large sums of money.

The crisis of 2008 defined Ben Bernanke's tenure in office. It took away much of the freedom any central banker enjoys during stable and

---

[2] In this interpretation, Bernanke was joining with prominent economic historians Barry Eichengreen and Peter Temin (see Bibliography), who highlighted the central role of the international gold standard in sustaining monetary rigidities. Although the international gold standard had long passed by the time Bernanke wrote these words, the Great Depression's historical lesson—about the need for central bank liquidity during several credit contractions—was better understood than ever, and recently had been demonstrated by Bernanke's predecessor, Alan Greenspan, during the Wall Street crash of 1987.

prosperous times, placing him more in a reactive than proactive mode. The crisis also defined his Fed chairmanship because of its severity and length; far from being a temporary jolt like the 1987 major correction that Greenspan confronted early in his term, 2008 was global in proportions and generated a long tail. By some measures, economic recovery in the U.S. took six years or more.

Bernanke's record regarding 2008 and its aftermath was decidedly mixed. It rightfully includes not only how the Federal Reserve responded once the collapse began, but also what its chairman thought and said in the months and years leading up to the collapse. Unfortunately, like his predecessor, chairman Bernanke saw conditions as essentially sound and failed to issue warnings or take measures to control excessive credit creation or derivatives. I still recall when he came over to my table following a lecture he delivered at New York University in 2007. "Well, Henry," he said, "I see you are still holding our feet to the fire." I replied, only half-jokingly, "But I don't see any smoke coming from your shoes."

Once the crisis hit, the Bernanke Fed was slow to respond. This is somewhat understandable, given the gravity of the situation. Eventually, the central bank began a regimen of quantitative easing that provided some economic stimulus. In addition to keeping interest rates close to zero, the Fed aggressively purchased mortgage-backed securities, Treasury bills, and other assets. Deciding that another round was needed in 2010, the Fed launched what became known as QE2 (for quantitative easing), which was followed by QE3 in 2012. While some warned that the economy was becoming addicted to such generous infusions, the retroactively named QE1 along with QE2 and QE3 at a minimum helped the so-called Great Recession from deepening and shortened its duration. In retrospect, then, Chairman Bernanke's failure to anticipate the crisis, to head it off, or to act promptly once it hit should be balanced against his interventions once he recognized its seriousness.

One reason for the lack of foresight about the crisis was that, like his predecessor at the helm of the Fed, Mr. Bernanke didn't understand the interrelationships between monetary policy and financial markets and institutions. This became more obvious to me when he gave a talk at the Economic Club of New York on November 16, 2009. For many years, the Club had designated me as one of two questioners when Fed chairmen spoke there. One of my questions to Ben Bernanke was: "Of all the information the Federal Reserve receives, what would you like to know that you do not know today." "Henry," he replied, "I would like to know what all that stuff is worth." He was referring to the financial assets in the marketplace—more and more of it neither traded in regulated markets nor listed on the balance sheets of corporations. In a similar vein, Bernanke asserted—just a few months before the collapse of Lehman Brothers in September 2008—that the mortgage securities problem was well contained.

Although Chairman Bernanke ultimately took steps (such as quantitative easing) to prevent the 2008 crisis from becoming much worse, his major shortcoming was on the front end of the crisis. As Adam Posen noted in his review essay on Bernanke's memoir in *Foreign Policy*, the "truly critical period" was the year before a landslide turned into an avalanche. "The Fed took little action after the bank BNP Paribas suspended three of its funds in August 2007 owing to troubles in the subprime mortgage market, or in the months that followed, as several U.S.-based lenders failed or were taken over." After Bear Stearns failed in March 2008, many feared for the fate of other major financial institutions. "Yet Bernanke's memoir ..." Posen observed, "presents no convincing evidence that the Fed undertook any policies in the following weeks or months to prevent that cascade" (Posen 2016, pp. 156–157).

After the fact, the Fed's refusal to rescue Lehman has been widely criticized. In his voluminous memoir, published seven years after the Lehman debacle, Ben Bernanke claims that no key player saw Lehman bankruptcy as an acceptable, much less the best, option. "In the many discussions in which I was involved," he assures his readers, "I never heard anyone from the Fed or the Treasury suggest that letting Lehman fail would be anything other than a disaster, or that we should contemplate allowing the firm to fail" (Bernanke 2015, p. 262).

And yet it did. Bernanke evokes a legalistic defense, asserting that "… neither the Fed nor the FDIC had the authority to take over Lehman, nor could the FDIC deposit funds be used to cover any losses. Legally, the government's only alternative, if Lehman couldn't find new capital, would have been trying to force the firm into bankruptcy." His explanation for why Lehman failed without Fed support was that it was found to be deeply insolvent and no suitable buyer had stepped forward from among the leading investment banks. "Even when invoking our 13(3) emergency authority," Bernanke wrote, "we were required to lend against adequate collateral."

Yet according to other authorities, including the author of a new study of the Fed's independence (Wharton Business School professor Peter Conti-Brown), the Fed applied 13(3) selectively and capriciously when it declined Lehman, then bailed out AIG just two days later. The 13(3) provision, Conti-Brown writes, contains

> no requirement that the institution be objectively solvent; the Reserve Bank only has to be satisfied with the collateral presented. And there is no requirement that "no one else would lend" [Bernanke's words]; there only

needed to be evidence—some evidence, any evidence—that other alternatives weren't "adequate." It is as broad a discretion that Congress could've written short of announcing that the Fed was in the business of giving away free money. (Conti-Brown 2016, p. 95)

The federal government's own National Commission on the Causes of the Financial and Economic Crisis in the United States reached the same basic conclusion in 2011. According to the Commission's Financial Crisis Inquiry Report, the decision of federal government officials to not rescue Lehman Brothers "added to uncertainty and panic in the financial markets." The report continues: "After the fact, they justified their decision by stating that the Federal Reserve did not have the legal authority to rescue Lehman" (Financial Crisis Inquiry Commission 2011, p. 343).

The decision by key government officials to let Lehman fail was heavily influenced by politics. The federal rescue of Bear Stearns (through the purchase by J.P. Morgan, with government assistance) the previous spring had generated severe discontent and political pressure. How could a Republican administration with a Republican-appointed treasury secretary (Hank Paulson) and Fed chairman sanction a government bailout of one of the private firms that had placed massive and, as it turned out, massively risky bets?

This question was very much alive when Lehman became one of the next major investment houses in danger of collapse. Indeed, Bernanke acknowledges in his memoir that Hank Paulson "didn't like being the public face of Wall Street bailouts," and recalls that he, Paulson, and other key officials faced "bitter criticism" from political, popular, and media corners over the prospect of a Lehman bailout (Bernanke 2015, pp. 260–261). As a former CEO of Goldman Sachs, Paulson well understood investment banking. But his press conferences throughout the

2008 crisis suggested shortcomings in his understanding of the intricacies of money and capital markets. At the same time, some critics accused him of being too friendly to Wall Street, especially in light of the Bear Stearns bailout.

Paulson outranked Bernanke in the government hierarchy, and he took the lead in the Lehman crisis. But from a legal perspective, the Fed was responsible for overseeing Lehman and other investment banking houses. The firm's fate came to a head on a Sunday evening (September 14, 2008). As a board member, I recall this key moment in financial history quite well. By 8:00 p.m. or so, the Lehman board was informed that the government would provide no financial assistance. Should the firm declare bankruptcy? Then the chairman of the Securities and Exchange Commission, Christopher Cox, called to ask for our decision. He urged us to act promptly because the financial markets in the Far East were about to reopen, and the uncertainty could roil global markets. During Cox's call, Secretary Paulson was with him, urging Cox to convince the Lehman board to vote for bankruptcy, even though Paulson had no legal authority over Cox. Paulson initially tried to put together a Lehman buyout by a consortium of banks headed by Barclays, but the British government supposedly forbade the deal, and some U.S. government officials claimed that Lehman lacked enough credit-worthy collateral to justify a federal rescue. Amid the tumultuous events of that evening, there was also a patriotic appeal to the board to approve bankruptcy in the interest of minimizing damage to the financial system.

I initially opposed bankruptcy, believing that if we kept the doors open, government officials would be compelled to come to the company's aid in one way or another. That was a riskier strategy; bankruptcy seemed more prudent to the majority of board members. I wasn't willing to follow a riskier path simply to save the company (or some version of it) for its own sake. Rather, I believed that bankruptcy would cause problems well beyond what the authorities were considering. And, unfortunately, with the bankruptcy, those problems followed in short order. The next day, AIG, which had taken very heavy positions in credit default insurance, nearly went under, although in that case the government stepped in to provide enormous support. Federal officials also found it necessary to support the creditworthiness of money market funds, to make large equity investments in commercial banks, and to institute a host of other measures.

Bernanke, Paulson, and other government officials who concluded that Lehman should declare bankruptcy seemingly misunderstood how financial assets are valued. The marketability of an asset is very fluid. What was marketable in spring 2008 was much less so by the fall. The financial crisis itself was a colossal demonstration of the declining marketability of financial assets through the process of contagion. The Bear Stearns case demonstrated this reality quite clearly, as did the weeks leading up to Lehman's bankruptcy.

The events of 2008 hold important lessons. Financial reporters are pressured to provide immediate analysis. Major participants seek to justify their actions. That is understandable, but not necessarily correct. It can often take years to gain the proper perspective on key events and actions. As noted, the Federal Commission on the 2008 crisis, Professor Conti-Brown, and other authorities have concluded that the Fed could have rescued Lehman. A recent study by Professor Laurence M. Ball, chairman of the economics department at Johns Hopkins University, offers the fullest analysis of the episode. Ball's major conclusions (see Fig. 5.1)—which diverge sharply from those of Paulson and Bernanke—are that policymakers failed to scrutinize Lehman's assets; that Lehman pos-

- There is a substantial record of policymakers' deliberations before the bankruptcy, and it contains no evidence that they examined the adequacy of Lehman's collateral, or that legal barriers deterred them from assisting the firm.

- Arguments about legal authority made by policymakers since the bankruptcy are unpersuasive.

- These arguments involve flawed interpretations of economic and legal concepts, and factual claims that do not appear to be accurate.

- From a *de novo* examination of Lehman's finances, it is clear that the firm had ample collateral for a loan to meet its liquidity needs. Such a loan could have prevented a disorderly bankruptcy, with negligible risk to the Fed.

- More specifically, Lehman probably could have survived by borrowing from the Fed's Primary Dealer Credit Facility on the terms offered to other investment banks. Fed officials prevented this outcome by restricting Lehman's access to the PDCF.

  We will never know what Lehman Brothers' long-term fate would have been if the Fed rescued it from its liquidity crisis. Lehman might have survived indefinitely as an independent firm; it might have been acquired by another institution; or eventually it might have been forced to wind down its business. Any of these outcomes, however, would likely have been less disruptive to the financial system than the bankruptcy that actually occurred.

  If legal constraints do not explain the non-rescue of Lehman, then what does? The available evidence supports the theories that political considerations were important, and that policymakers did not fully anticipate the damage from the bankruptcy. The record also shows that the decision to let Lehman fail was made primarily by Treasury Secretary Henry Paulson. Fed officials deferred to Paulson even though they had sole authority to make the decision under the Federal Reserve Act.

Fig. 5.1 "The Fed and Lehman Brothers": Major conclusions of the Laurence Ball report

sessed adequate collateral; that no legal barriers prevented the Fed from lending to the bank; and that several options beside bankruptcy were available, all of them probably less damaging. The failure of Lehman was the linchpin that brought global finance to its knees. In a later chapter (Chap. 13), I discuss the risks when the Federal Reserve bows to political pressure. There is no better example than the failure of Lehman Brothers.

It is much too early to objectively evaluate the performance of the new Fed chair, Janet Yellen, who was nominated by President Obama and sworn in February 2014. Yellen came into her current position with very strong credentials: a Ph.D. in economics from Yale University, a professorship at the University of California, former Chair of the President's Council of Economic Advisers (1997–1999), President of the Federal Reserve Bank of San Francisco (2004–2010), and Vice Chair of the Fed's Board of Governors (2010–2014). She also made history as the first woman to head the central bank.

One of Yellen's strengths at the helm of the Fed has been her leadership style. So far no meaningful opposition to her views has emerged. On the margins, only a few Governors have voted against her on monetary matters. As noted (see Ch. 4), this is in sharp contrast to the opposition Paul Volcker sometimes confronted within his Board. More than that, it doesn't appear that Yellen has achieved strong consensus by subordinating her views to the wishes of the Federal Open Market Committee.

Like her predecessor, Chairwoman Yellen has been a strong supporter of the Fed's practice of providing forward guidance. This is not a plus, in my view, for I remain convinced that the central bank's economic and financial projections—which sometime reach as long as three years into the future—distort financial market behavior. Forward guidance encourages market participants to speculate and to take excessive market risks. But long-term guidance has not been, nor should anyone expect it to be, very accurate. Meanwhile, the Fed assumes that its forecasts are based on reasonable financial market responses.

Dr. Yellen and many of her Fed colleagues also remain largely wedded to analyses of economic and financial events through a cyclical prism—that is, the modeling of economic and financial actions based on historical data. Cyclical overlays are analytically comforting, but have severe limitations. Most importantly: they do not offer insight into the structural changes that continue to transform financial markets and the larger economy. That is why previous Fed chairmen such as Alan Greenspan and Ben Bernanke failed to take preventative actions to rein in speculative excesses, and ultimately were blindsided. The same was true for Yellen when she was President of the Federal Reserve Bank of San Francisco and Vice Chair of the Fed.

With the advent of the Trump administration, tectonic shifts loom ahead for the management and conduct of monetary policy. As this book goes to press, market participants are speculating about who might replace Janet Yellen as the next head of the Federal Reserve. Although quite unpredictable, president-elect Trump was, while candidate Trump, highly critical of Mrs. Yellen, so there is a very good chance she will become one of only two post-World War Fed chairs to not serve more than one term. (William Miller did not finish his first term.) Moreover, several Fed chairmen were reappointed by presidents not of their own party affiliation: Bill Martin, Paul Volcker, Alan Greenspan, and Ben Bernanke.

What credentials will President Trump look for in selecting the next Federal Reserve chair? In the post-World War II era, most top central bankers were noted trained economists, including Burns, Volcker, Greenspan, Bernanke, and Yellen. In contrast, William Martin, the longest-running Fed chairman, was not a trained economist per se but brought a mixture of business and government experience to the position; and William

Miller had been head of Textron, an industrial conglomerate. He proved to be unable to cope with hyperinflation in the late 1970s. Will the new president seek out another economist with political and economic persuasions similar to his own, or search for someone with a broader and less technical background in economics and finance? Mr. Trump's record of staffing his cabinet and major government agencies to date suggests he is not likely to appoint a Federal Reserve chair who is steeped in monetary traditions or in the tactics and language of central bank policy.

His influence on the central bank won't stop there. Along with nominating a new Fed chair, Mr. Trump will have the opportunity to replace most of the central bank's senior management in short order. On the seven-person Board of Governors (of which the chairman is a member), there are already two vacancies that the new president can fill immediately. Stanley Fisher, whose term as vice chairman will expire in June 2018, may well step down before his term expires. Several other Board members may also retire before the end of their terms. This is not unusual. In the past, few Fed Governors have served out their fourteen-year terms. It seems to me, therefore, that within the next two years or so, the new administration will need to replace at least five of the several Governors of the Board. Even though many new Governors have been drawn in recent decades from the ranks of economists, with quite a few coming from the staff of the Fed itself, I doubt that approach will continue.

In view of these likely sweeping changes in the Fed's senior management, monetary policy strategy and tactics will change as well. Forward guidance—one of the dominant current features of monetary policy— almost surely will not survive. Federal Reserve projections of economic activity several years into the future have not been very accurate because they have been based on past cyclical economic overlays that failed to take into consideration structural changes in the economy and in financial markets. Going forward, Fed guidelines are likely to be broader and less definitive than in recent years.

The financial challenges facing the new president are not of his own making, but they will be front and center as he takes office. Some are unavoidable. There is an overloaded debt structure in all sectors of the U.S. economy and financial markets. Financial assets are concentrated to an unprecedented degree within a small number of too-big-to-fail institutions. And our financial system has become overly dependent on the Federal Reserve as a source of liquidity.

6

Charles Sanford and the Rise
of Quantitative Risk Management

Charles "Charlie" Sanford, Jr., was one of the most innovative, entre-preneurial, and philosophical commercial bankers in the post-World War II era. Although little remembered today, he was a pivotal figure in recent financial history who was central to bringing about a tectonic shift in modern commercial banking. He did this by transforming Bankers Trust Company from a commercial bank into a merchant-investment bank. More broadly, he put in place innovative quantitative risk management techniques as the principal tool for assessing risks—tools that became widespread throughout the industry. But his career was check-ered. During his tenure at Bankers Trust, the bank's balance sheet was restructured and profits rose sharply. Yet by the time Sanford retired in 1997, profits were declining and the bank was embroiled in litigation.

The Sanford story of rise and decline parallels and contributed to larger trends in post-World War II U.S. banking: a growing sense that tradi-

© The Author(s) 2016
H. Kaufman, *Tectonic Shifts in Financial Markets*,
DOI 10.1007/978-3-319-48387-0_6

tional commercial banking was outmoded and boring; the rise of more aggressive risk-taking; the development of new techniques for measuring and controlling risk, many of which proved to be hollow; and the limitations of senior managers of diversified financial institutions over the complex operations of their firms. Charlie Sanford's case is especially intriguing because he thought and wrote a great deal about the place of banking in our society as a vital service. He was, to borrow a term from management studies, a "reflective practitioner."

Bankers Trust was founded in 1903 by a group of New York banks. It was headed by steel executive Edmund C. Converse, with voting power held by three partners in the J.P. Morgan firm. Bankers Trust was designed as a "bankers' bank" in the sense that it would provide trust services to other banks across the country (while not competing for their commercial customers) and serve as a repository for capital that member banks could draw on as needed. The institution played a key role in J. Pierpont Morgan's interventions during the Panic of 1907, and a few years later acquired two other leading trust companies, Mercantile Trust and Manhattan Trust. In 1914, Benjamin Strong, Jr.—then emerging as one of the nation's leading bankers after helping found the U.S. Federal Reserve—served as second president of Bankers Trust for a short while before becoming head of the Federal Reserve Bank of New York. Although Bankers Trust downsized to conform to the Glass-Steagall Act of 1933, its trust department remained intact.

Following the Second World War, Bankers Trust made some additional acquisitions but remained a staid institution. That began to change in 1980, when, under CEO Alfred Brittain III, Bankers Trust began to sell off its retail banking operations. By that time, a young executive was rising in the ranks who would eventually transform the institution even more.

Charles Steadman Sanford, Jr., earned an undergraduate degree in 1958 from the University of Georgia, where his family had long ties. (His father also was a graduate, and his grandfather had served as the university's president.) Charlie went on to complete an MBA at the University of Pennsylvania's Wharton School, yet he and his wife remained deeply committed to his undergraduate alma mater.

Charlie joined Bankers Trust in 1961 as a commercial banking officer. I became aware of him about a decade later, when he hired Alan Lerner, an economist whom I had recruited to Salomon Brothers in 1972. Alan was teaching at NYU and close to completing a Ph.D. I assigned him the task of closely monitoring the Fed and the US Treasury. I transferred this responsibility to him because of my broader research and firm responsibilities I had assumed being part of the firm's senior management. Alan carried out his task extremely well. I was sorry to lose him, while Sanford sensed that Alan would fit into the Bank's new risk-oriented activities extremely well. Alan flourished at Bankers, but left the bank in 1994. I suspect he was unhappy with the manner and magnitude of the quantitative risk-taking arrangements and with the growing disregard for client relationships.

I got to know Charlie somewhat more personally when he became the fourth member of our Foursome luncheon. He was a member for about four years and left our luncheon group when he retired from Bankers in 1997. He did not give the appearance of a typical head of a large financial institution. He was courteous and unassuming. Despite his position, he lived in a nice but hardly ostentatious home in the suburbs. He drove an understated car in keeping, I suspect, with his other parsimonious spending habits.

***

Sanford found his calling in 1969, when he was transferred to the Resource Management Department at Bankers Trust. That unit handled government bonds, municipal bonds, foreign exchange, and other short-term instruments, but also was responsible for funding the bank and managing its investment account. After Charlie became the head of the department, he was largely responsible for formulating and instituting a quantitative procedure labeled RAROC, for Risk Adjusted Return On Capital. The technique eventually was applied to many different bank asset classes, modified to suit each asset class. As Deutsche Bank Managing Director Gene Guill later explained, in tracing the development of risk management, Sanford's models factored in "the expected utilization of the loan, the credit rating of the borrower, the maturity, the credit duration, the commitment fee and the net interest margin" (Guill 2009, p. 13).

As Sanford later described the approach:

> We treated the market as if it were efficient over a two-week time frame. Inside that period we (the dealer) could see supply and demand characteristics more perceptibly than did non-dealers. We designed our customer base to be a sample of the market. Using the information we got from that base, we were able to assess value. At the same time, we began using the laws of probability on a much finer scale than they had been used before. This was the beginning of the risk management revolution that we brought to the fore in the 1980s. (Sanford 1996)

By deploying models that relied on duration, probabilities, and mark-to-market values, Sanford's unit was for the first time attempting to assess risk comprehensively, taking into account all assets and liabilities, including off-balance-sheet. In this way, Sanford reflected, "Bankers Trust became the first financial institution to explicitly quantify risks in a framework that allowed management to make better risk/return tradeoffs in a real business setting" (Sanford 1996). It was a milestone in American financial history.

With the new metrics in hand, Bankers Trust restructured its balance sheet accordingly. The bank began to participate actively in a loan market in which originators shared a portion of the loan exposure with other lenders, which not only reduced the exposure for Bankers Trust but also freed up more of its capital for additional loans. This was a prudent strategy. But far less prudent was the firm's aggressive move into both leveraged buyouts and financial derivatives. Those two markets, of course, would come to exemplify a Wall Street culture of aggressive risk taking and, at least in the case of derivatives, out-of-control complexity—a culture that contributed centrally to the financial collapse of 2008.

But at this early stage they generated staggering profits. By steering the company into LBOs, derivatives, and other emerging markets, Sanford's formulas seemed almost like an Aladdin's lamp. Between the 1968–1977 and the 1978–1987 decades, return on equity at Bankers Trust grew from 10.4 percent to 13.3 percent, while net income (after tax) soared from $57 million to $220 million. Charlie Sanford became chairman and CEO of Bankers Trust in 1987. Now firmly at the helm, he pushed the new strategy even more aggressively. In the next ten years (to 1988–1997), ROE jumped to 16.5 percent, and net income skyrocketed to $506 million.

The fact that the bank's soaring profits were chiefly driven by risk arbitraging techniques is revealed in a different set of figures. The bank was getting out of the business of traditional lending. When Sanford became CEO and chairman, the bank's ratio of loans to total assets was 60 percent. When he stepped down in 1997, the ratio had fallen to 10 percent. But there were troubling undercurrents. In 1987, the company took charge-offs totaling $636 million that reduced net income to only $1.2 million. According to analysis by Gene Guill, these loans were booked before August 1982. They had been originated by the International Credit Group of the International Department, which did not report to Sanford and were not subject to his risk management discipline. Nevertheless, the widely reported public numbers made Bankers Trust a darling of Wall Street.

In 1993, Sanford penned what became his most well-known speech. It was an impressive demonstration of his sharp and restless intellect. In "Financial Markets in 2020," Sanford etched a vision of the future in which financial analysis drew on quantum physics, molecular biology, chaos theory, fuzzy logic, neural networks, and other advanced fields in the sciences to better balance risk and return. Most Wall Streeters had not heard of these arcane theories, much less imagine their relevance to finance and economics. But Sanford's future was hardly dehumanized or dystopian. In his characteristically humanistic way, he sought to meld high science with human judgment and wisdom. In "particle finance," as he called it, "the financial professional who prices the risk attributes will continue to use a combination of automated analytics and judgment." And the sophisticated new science of finance would offer broad benefits.

A social critic may say they are nothing more than a financial engineering exercise designed to enrich a few at the expense of many—a zero-sum game. Not true. For as risk management becomes ever more precise and customized, the amount of risk that we all have to bear will be greatly reduced, lowering the need for financial capital. This will have a tremendous social value because financial capital that had been required to cushion these risks will be available elsewhere in society to produce more wealth to address society's needs. In addition, this will liberate human capital by the greater leveraging of talent. (Sanford 1993b)

The year before his 1997 retirement, riding a wave of success, Sanford gave an address at the Wharton School in which he reflected on not only quantitative risk management innovations at Bankers Trust, but also their broad social and moral implications. He valued, he said, innovation and creativity, effective leadership, breaking free of past conventions, and ethical behavior. Market participants should not pursue gain narrowly, but rather should "develop a sense of the value of a financial instrument as opposed to just its price—because this leads to a more efficient allocation of resources." And that, in turn, would "create wealth for society—because this leads to a higher standard of living (both material and non-material for all people)." Indeed, the non-material mattered as much or more than the material, in Sanford's framework. For all should strive, he said, for balance in life through family and cultural and spiritual interests outside of business (Sanford 1997).

The financial tide turned for the bank in 1998, when net (after tax) income fell from the previous year's $506 million to a loss of $73 million. This became a flood the following year, with losses of nearly $2 billion. These losses were driven by the very activities Charlie had pioneered and propelled forward as head of the bank.

Even before these huge reported losses, Bankers Trust had been sued by at least two major clients for allegedly misleading them or concealing information from them about derivatives risks the bank took with their investment capital. Investigations led to some very troubling revelations, fines, and legal troubles that put the bank in a precarious position. As *Business Week* reported: "It's November 2, 1993, and two employees of Bankers Trust Co. are discussing a leveraged derivative deal the bank had recently sold to Procter & Gamble Co. '... They would never be able to know how much money was taken out of that,' says one employee referring to the huge profit the bank stood to make on the transaction. 'Never, no way, no way,' replies her colleague. 'That's the beauty of Bankers Trust.'"

Then, in early 1995, the *New York Times* reported that "[l]ast month, when [Bankers Trust] agreed to pay a $10 million fine to settle charges that it had hidden the extent of Gibson Greetings Inc.'s losses from trading derivatives, it was more than an embarrassment and wrist-slap from Federal regulators." According to an SEC document, a Bankers Trust executive was recorded telling a colleague that he had lied to Gibson about losses. "We told him $8.2 million when the real number was $14 million," the executive recounted bluntly ("Business Day" 1995).

Had Sanford sanctioned or encouraged such actions on the part of his investors and risk managers? I doubt it. My personal interactions with Charlie over the years suggest an ethical man who saw social benefits flowing from sound corporate behavior. So do his writings and pronouncements. This, however, does not absolve Sanford for his inability to manage effectively the individuals under his command. The CEO is the ultimate risk manager of the firm. That responsibility cannot be assigned to anyone else. As the chief strategist, the CEO holds responsibility for the firm's capital allocation. More specifically, in Charlie's case, was his failure over time to insist that his senior managers put client relationships above near-term gains. That in turn caused those who thought otherwise to lose influence within the bank, and several—including Alan Lerner— eventually left. Ironically, Lerner and his like-minded cohort were trying to abide by Charlie's high ideals.

Charles Sanford certainly possessed an idealistic view of capitalism and the functioning of competitive markets. He aspired to make Bankers Trust a model that could be emulated by other financial institutions. He conceived of wealth broadly to encompass "everything that can be defined as useful or agreeable in serving a human purpose, including well-being, happiness, and prosperity." He longed for a civilized society, but one in which individuals are diverse, expressive, and imperfect rather than ideal. The Golden Rule in one form or another, he inveighed, is a "value of all great religious and ethical traditions and applies to all regardless of their station in life" (Sanford 1993a).

Sanford was even more specific when it came to Bankers Trust employees. In a 1997 address entitled "Social Contract," he asserted that

> We have high standards in every way. In addition to placing high value on others we stress intellectual honesty in all our decisions. Intellectual honesty is more than what's legislated—it is inherent in the best people, those who take a broader view than simply 'What's in it for me?' ... [At Bankers Trust there is] no pressure to behave unethically .... [We expect] ethical behavior with no exception, ever, not only as mandated by regulators but also by intellectual honesty—by the relentless application of sound judgment and critical thinking to any undertaking performed on behalf of Bankers Trust. (Sanford 1992)

The contrast between what Charlie Sanford tried to create at Bankers Trust and its ethical and legal travails must have been a great disappointment to him. He tried to instill a high ethical standard into an environment of rapid transactions, increasingly distant client relationships, and enormous profit potential. Ironically, although the risk management techniques he helped pioneer held the potential for reducing volatility in financial markets, their highly complex, technical nature made them just as often tools for greater obscurity rather than greater transparency. Moreover, as Gene Guill concluded in his analysis of the development of risk management at Bankers Trust: "One of the biggest dangers with models is that users may arise to challenge them by failing to question their assumptions, their parameters, and their specifications. Over time, variables and relationships that were originally thought to be significant or simply ignored may become highly significant and the model itself may produce misleading results."

I suspect an even greater challenge for risk management is that senior managers tend to marginalize warnings from their risk managers, especially during bullish times. Senior managers are loath to lower shareholder expectations. This places those charged with the management of risk in a precarious position, tactically and politically. They are disadvantaged in the eyes of senior management relative to leading traders and other "rain makers." Even though risk management had become fairly commonplace among leading financial institutions by the end of the twentieth century, its practitioners were often ignored by their bosses in the run-up to 2008.

These dynamics were described by the former chief credit officer and chief risk officer at Washington Mutual Bank, which collapsed in 2008 because of its heavy involvement in sub-prime and adjustable rate mortgage lending. During his time at WaMu (1999–2005), James G. Vanasek had issued repeated warnings about and proposals to rein in the company's exorbitant risk taking, according to his 2010 testimony before the U.S. Senate's Permanent Subcommittee on Investigations. "In many ways and on many occasions I attempted to limit what was happening." He proposed capping the percentage of sub-prime and high risk loans in the portfolio. He tried to limit the number of stated-income loans (that is, loans made without borrower income verification). "Loan originators constantly threatened to quit and go to Countrywide or elsewhere," he recalled, "if their loan applications were not approved." When the company adopted "The Power of Yes" as its mortgage marketing slogan, he called for a counterbalancing "The Wisdom of No." The proposal ran so counter to the prevailing culture that "many considered my statement exceedingly risky from a career perspective," Vanasek testified. Neither these nor Vanasek's other risk-limiting proposals garnered strong top management support (Vanasek 2010). With assets valued at nearly $329 billion (in 2007), Washington Mutual's failure was the largest in U.S. banking history.

It would be wonderful if Sanford's vision of finance would come to fruition soon. I doubt it, especially because the financial sector should aspire to even higher standards of behavior than the broader business arena. This is because financial institutions hold in trust our savings and temporary funds. They hold the savings and temporary funds of all of us. They are, therefore, guardians. If they go astray, we all suffer, individually and as an economic democracy. Rules of responsible financial behavior are, therefore, essential. What they should be and how they should be enforced remains the thorny issue of our day. The financial world envisioned by Charlie Sanford is highly desirable, but would require huge leaps to come about.

The vision of finance in 2020 that Sanford sketched out in 1993 has in fact turned out quite differently. Although finance has become much more technical and scientific in the two decades since Sanford's creative speech, it has not been tempered enough by human judgment; modeling has become king. More than that, although capital reserves have shrunken on average since 1993, this has not happened because risk is better controlled but because risk has become more generally acceptable and systemic.

Following Sanford's retirement, new Bankers Trust leaders attempted to revert back to more traditional banking practices. In November 1998, Deutsche Bank voted to acquire Bankers Trust for $10.1 billion. It was a lifesaver, because before the sale was finalized, Bankers Trust pleaded guilty in an escheatment lawsuit, which banned the institution (as a convicted felon) from trading several categories of securities. Left on its own, Bankers Trust would have vanished completely. After several more years, Deutsche Bank sold the (former Bankers Trust) trust and custody division to State Street Bank.

Judging by what would happen in 2008, the financial community ignored or quickly forgot important lessons—about risk management, corporate culture, and ethical financial behavior—from the rise and fall of Bankers Trust under Charles Sanford.

7

The Dominance of Walter Wriston

During the Second World War and for several more years, financial managers adjusted to the new rules and regulations put into place during the New Deal and began to finance the private sector again. But over time the legacy of financial excess in the 1920s faded. By the 1960s, managers and owners who had dominated during the Great Depression were retired or fired, giving way to a new generation of financial leaders. Within that generation, the most dominant banker was Walter Wriston of Citibank. More than any other figure, Wriston—as CEO of one of the world's largest financial institutions from 1967 to 1984—pushed the boundaries of American banking. No one, thus far, has been his equal.

Wriston was neither a trained economist nor a business school graduate, but rather held a Master's degree from the Tufts University Fletcher School of Law and Diplomacy, where his early ambition was to pursue a career in diplomacy. His father had been a well-known academic leader as

© The Author(s) 2016

H. Kaufman, *Tectonic Shifts in Financial Markets*,

DOI 10.1007/978-3-319-48387-0_7

president of Lawrence College and Brown University. After serving in the military in World War II, Wriston was unsure he could make a career in diplomacy and, with some prodding and an introduction to the National City Bank (today Citi), he started his banking career in 1946 with a salary of $2500 per year. He learned banking the hard way—by rotating through many divisions within the bank, domestically and internationally. By the time he rose to CEO in July 1967, he had established a strong managerial imprint and a distinctive public persona.

At the height of his power, Wriston was quite imposing. A tall man, he possessed a steely demeanor and an acerbic personality. Although he assembled a talented group of top managers, reliable reports suggested that relations at the senior level of his bank were far from harmonious. He was politically connected at high levels in Washington, and known for delivering well-crafted speeches.

Yet it was ultimately the quality of his ideas rather than the force of his personality or his outspokenness that mattered most, and there the reality often failed to live up to the rhetoric. Under Wriston, Citibank loaned heavily in Latin America, with near disastrous results. He also pushed aggressively on several other fronts—as a leading proponent of removing the barriers to interstate banking, of lifting the interest rate ceilings paid by banks (through negotiable certificates of deposit and other means), and of aggressively promoting credit cards. Under Wriston, Citibank invented the ATM (Automatic Teller Machine) and dotted the landscape with the kiosks, for both cost-cutting and customer convenience.

Three of Wriston's core beliefs drove much of the bank's strategy and, in turn, influenced the larger landscape of postwar commercial banking. He was committed to the notion that Citibank should and could increase annual earnings by 15 percent. It was an audacious goal, and of course one that required extremely aggressive risk taking. One way to help achieve high profitability—Wriston's second core belief—was to roll back capital requirements. According to Wriston, banks no longer needed to hold capital as a percentage of liabilities at rates as high as in the past. In addition, Wriston was fond of saying that countries do not fail, which helped justify Citi's aggressive Latin American lending. He was apparently ignorant of, or at any rate dismissed, John Maynard Keynes's astute observation that "If you owe your bank a hundred pounds, you have a problem. But if you owe a million, it has."

Wriston's philosophical orientation and his bank's competitive strategies had profound influence on other financial institutions, large and small. In my view, however, he was a kind of Pied Piper of the financial marketplace, as quite a few institutions tried to emulate his policies and practices, many to their ultimate dismay. I disagreed with his overall approach and with many of his observations, and he disagreed with mine.

One of these differences surfaced in 1976. I had been asked to give a talk sponsored by the *Financial Times*. The title of my speech was, "Will the Bankers Need to Adjust To a Harsher Climate Over the Longer Term?" One of my conclusions was that during the past decade "a new generation of business managers began to believe that instant and permanent success could be attained through financial leverage, conglomeration, synergism and congenerics .... [At the same time, banks moved] to liberate themselves from constraints [and participated in] broader efforts to free up the entire financial system." I specifically pointed to negotiable certificates of deposit (as noted, a hallmark of Citibank's strategy). "What appeared at first blush to be a highly favorable backdrop for banking in the early 1970s," I concluded, "resulted in rather harsh consequences."

My remarks garnered considerable public attention but did not resonate well at Citibank. I was asked to have lunch with some of the firm's senior managers, including Wriston, Edward Palmer (chairman of the bank's Executive Committee), and William Ira Spencer. The Citi men clearly disapproved of my analysis. In particular, they argued that I didn't evaluate correctly the new fundamentals of banking. In their view, it was essential to lock in the spread between the cost of bank liabilities and the return on assets. This was now possible, they continued, largely through the issuance of negotiable CDs and floating rate financing, which reduced the need for bank capital. Wriston believed that spread banking liberated the banks from interest rate constraints.

My rebuttal focused on three points. First, in their world the task of imposing monetary restraint would require substantial increases in interest rates. Second, continued resistance to monetary restraint would encourage the ongoing financing of marginal borrowers. Third, that in turn would produce widening yield spreads between high- and low-quality debt and thus cause a banking and monetary policy problem. The men around the table refuted each of these points. As one put it: "Henry, we are bankers and know how to make credit judgments." History, of course, has proven otherwise.

While public comments by Wriston about me were, for many years, limited, he was reported to have said at one of the meetings of the Business Council that "Kaufman was right on interest rates about one time out of six." It was an outlandish remark without substance. Wriston's criticism of my economic and financial analysis came into full view when the *Wall Street Journal* asked him to review my first book, *Interest Rates, the Markets, and the New Financial World* (Kaufman 1986). He did not spare the rod. His opening salvo reflects both the vigor of his convictions and his witty sarcasm: "For Henry Kaufman, a senior officer of Salomon Brothers with a clear view of its trading floor, to deplore the creations of 'excess' credit is like a piano player in a fancy house protesting that he didn't know what was going on upstairs."

Although Wriston praised my chapter on fallen financial dogmas, and grudgingly acknowledged that "when he discusses interest rate trends, Mr. [not Dr.] Kaufman's analytical powers are everywhere evident," he struggled to find any other merit in the book. Instead, with typically colorful—indeed, at times exaggerated—prose, Wriston dubbed my concerns about aggressive commercial banking intrusions into investment banking "unseemly"; and erroneously said that my reservations about sole reliance on monetary policy meant that I saw monetarism as "a failed theory." Writing in 1986, Wriston was still a big fan of supply-side economics, chiding me for my criticism of what later independent analysis has shown to be an unsuccessful doctrine (Fullerton 1994). What most rankled Citibank's chief ambassador, however, was my central argument that credit markets functioned better with a "guardian" and that, as Wriston aptly summarized my position, "deregulation threatens the whole financial system, besides having other undesirable effects." He would have none of it. Wriston died three years before the 2008 financial crisis. It would have been interesting to hear his explanation.

It would be overreaching to suggest that Walter Wriston was the sole architect of the sweeping liberalization of banking from the mid-1960s to the mid-1980s and beyond. Regulators played a major role as well. But they were pushed and prodded on many fronts by Wriston and his behemoth institution. No other commercial banker of the era was more outspoken, aggressive, or influential. No private figure was more responsible for the late twentieth century tectonic shift in commercial banking.

Citibank reached its high-water mark as an institution under Wriston. And financial liberalization did offer some benefits, especially for savers and investors who were offered a new range of products.

Yet Wriston and his colleagues remained blind to the other side of the equation—the reality that aggressive market liberalization injected new forms of risk into the financial system. Wriston sowed many of the seeds at Citi that later bore bitter fruit. His successor, John Reed, continued many of the same policies and practices. In turn, Weill's successor as CEO (in 2003) and chairman (2006), Charles "Chuck" Prince, also carried forward the Wriston mentality.

"As long as the music is playing," Prince told the *Financial Times*, when asked about the bank's aggressive lending for LBOs and other private equity deals, "you've got to get up and dance. We are all dancing." That was in July 2007, when Bear Stearns announced the collapse of two of its hedge funds and demand for mortgage-related securities was imploding.

Prince's comment struck me as a troubling indicator of excessive yet self-conscious risk taking on the part of financial leaders, so I wrote a column in the London *Financial Times* on why financial institutions felt compelled to lend even more into an already bloated credit market. The column's cautionary title was "Watch Your Step in the Liquidity Polka" (July 21, 2007). "Today," I noted, "companies and households alike often blur the distinction between liquidity and credit availability." Aggressive securitization was one driver. "The sharp increase in tradable assets has stimulated risk appetites, eroded traditional concepts of liquidity and fostered the expectation that credit is always available at reasonable prices." Technological advancements (such as computerized trading and near-instantaneous information flows) also was driving the trend by "encourag[ing] the notion that markets for credit are always available and with near-perfect information."

> No big financial institution wants to step off the dance floor while the music of liquidity is still playing. Doing so prematurely would risk the loss of enormous profits to competitors, declining earnings, eroding market share, employee dissatisfaction with bonuses and disgruntled shareholders. Executives are therefore loath to rely on judgment and reason in risk management. Rather, they are driven towards risk quantification and modeling, with their clear-cut timelines, aura of scientific certitude and lure of near-term profits.

This was hardly a message Wriston or Prince was eager to hear. In time, as the 2008 crisis worsened, Prince's words came back to haunt him, and to symbolize a financial meltdown propelled by reckless lending.

Among Citi's shortcomings, its poor control of risk-taking looms largest. And that affected other commercial banks, which felt the competitive pressure to diversify beyond their domain and take on higher risk as well. In commercial banking, Citi led the way in defining an expanded role for commercial banking.

8

The Bigness Crisis

While Wall Street, policymakers, and the nation as a whole watched the drama of the 2008 crisis unfold, fearful of systemic collapse, another drama was unfolding on the same stage. The institutions that intermediate between lenders and borrowers were collapsing and concentrating into a small number of super-dominant players. The process, in fact, was aided and abetted during the crisis by official policymakers. By then it was abundantly clear that the largest institutions were "too-big-to-fail." In an effort to minimize insolvency and market disruptions, Fed and other officials actually *encouraged* financial institutions to consolidate. They also required large institutions to accept an equity injection by the government itself. It was another way—one largely overlooked amid the crisis atmosphere—that the most severe financial crisis since the Great Depression damaged not only the financial system but also the larger economy.

© The Author(s) 2016
H. Kaufman, *Tectonic Shifts in Financial Markets*,
DOI 10.1007/978-3-319-48387-0_8

Concentration is a growing problem throughout the U.S. economy. In many sectors we are rapidly moving toward tight oligopolies. In 2015, a mere 6 percent of the Fortune 500—just twenty-eight companies—garnered more than half the total net income of firms in the index (Krantz 2016). The problem is especially acute in the financial sector.

Today we face a critical need for new regulation to address the current and future role of financial conglomerates—or, as some call them, integrated financial institutions. As debt has grown exponentially and as the financial systems have teetered close to collapse, financial authorities have given most of their attention to financial instruments—such as derivatives, mortgage-backed securities, and credit default swaps—and relatively little to the structure of dominant financial institutions.

Massive financial concentration seemed quite unlikely in the early post World War II years. The Great Depression that followed the speculative excesses of the 1920s inspired a sweeping political backlash (see Chap. 11). Congress passed a wave of tough legislation that constrained financial institutions, chiefly banks, within specified markets and segregated them from many activities. Financial conglomerates not only became unfashionable; they were outlawed. For their part, senior managers at most leading financial institutions still recalled vividly the harrowing banking failures and massive debt write-offs of the Depression years. It was reasonable to expect that financial specialization—with its segmented and well-defined borders—would last forever.

The consolidation of the American financial markets increased gradually, almost imperceptibly, in the 1960s and 1970s. It centered mainly on the mergers of banking institutions, especially among deposit-type institutions such as commercial banks and savings and loan associations. Many of the institutions that lost their independence through mergers had fallen victim to excessively liberal lending practices, a harbinger of the future.

The competitive pressures of the late 1970s and 1980s led to a wave of deregulation that essentially dismantled the New Deal Era regulatory regime. By the 1990s, financial concentration reached tidal wave proportions. The lynchpin was the abandonment of the Glass-Steagall Act, which had kept most financial businesses separate. At the time, official supervisors and regulators did not seem to grasp the ramifications—from risk contagion to conflicts of interest—of lowering the firewalls between financial sectors.

Consider some of the data on recent U.S. financial consolidation. As recently as 1990, the ten largest financial companies held about 10 percent of U.S. financial assets. Today they hold about 80 percent. Of the fifteen largest U.S. financial institutions in 1991, all but five have lost their independence as they were merged into the survivors. As for investment banking, only two organizations of significant size remain independent—Goldman Sachs and Morgan Stanley—and they rushed for cover during the chaos of fall 2008 under the Fed's umbrella to restructure into traditional bank holding companies. The list of key institutions that are no longer independent, some with names that have vanished, is a remarkable roster: E. F. Hutton, Kidder Peabody, Paine Webber, Dean Witter Reynolds, Merrill Lynch, Salomon Brothers, First Boston, Shearson Lehman, Drexel Burnham, Bache & Co., and Bear Stearns.

Today, large financial conglomerates are so diverse and integrated that to classify them along traditional lines as commercial banks, insurance companies, or investment banks would be misleading. Many provide deposit facilities within their holding company. Quite a few are active in the U.S. and abroad in a wide range of activities that includes investment banking, the trading of securities, proprietary trading, insurance, money market funds, and money management.

In my previous book, I tried to provide a broader (though far-from-complete) look at the market involvement of the fifteen largest financial institutions according to 2007 data. I added together their stated assets, off-balance sheet guarantees or commitments, gross notional derivatives underwritten, and assets under management for others. Together, these totaled $243 trillion. To be sure, these are not all liabilities but rather one rough measure of financial market involvement. Considering that the same fifteen top institutions had a total stated capital of only $837 billion, the order of magnitude of their reach into financial markets—whatever its precise dimensions—is staggering.

In light of such considerations, along with what we have learned through the travails of recent years, several conclusions about large financial institutions seem indisputable.

First, they have not been an anchor of stability in our financial system. It seems fair to say that if the federal government had not provided enormous amounts of direct and indirect financial support in key markets, all would have failed—even the healthier institutions would have been pulled down by their interconnections with weaker players. And that collapse, in turn, would have been followed by a harrowing economic depression.

Second, the top firms drove the credit creation process with great ingenuity and force. Their large and skilled management teams were at the forefront of securitization, propelling markets for derivatives, credit default swaps, mortgage-backed securities, and other exotic instruments to unprecedented scale and new levels of risk. They also played a central role in popularizing quantitative risk analysis techniques—techniques that, rather than controlling risk, tended to encourage risk-taking and contribute to debt overload.

Third, leading financial conglomerates played a central role in shifting the concept of liquidity to one that was asset-based to the liability side of the balance sheet. Years ago, liquidity at business corporations meant the size of liquid assets, the maturity of receivables, the turnover of inventory, and the relationship of these assets to total liabilities. For households it primarily meant the maturing assets being held for contingencies. But in recent decades, liquidity has increasingly come to mean access to credit. The dominant financial conglomerates were instrumental in this transformation—by aggressively marketing credit cards, by popularizing an array of new liberal mortgage financing techniques, and by spinning off many risky business and household assets into subsidiaries or securitizing them.

Fourth, there is a clear correlation between institutional bigness and rule breaking. According to the non-partisan CCP Research Foundation (UK), in the five years beginning 2010, a mere sixteen of the world's leading lenders racked up more than $300 billion in fines, settlements, and provisions related to financial wrongdoing (McClannahan 2015; McCormick 2015). Much of this troubling record, it seems to me, stems from the conflicts of interest inherent in financial conglomerates that too often operate on both sides of trades and offer consulting and auditing services to their own clients. The giants claim that vertical integration offers economies of scale and allows them to serve customers better through one-stop shopping. There is little or no evidence of the former, and while the latter may be true, the cost of convenience for financial markets is diminished competitiveness.

The Fed has failed to recognize that abandoning the Glass–Steagall Act would accelerate financial concentration and create more institutions deemed "too-big-to-fail." It is revealing that Fed officials never publicly admitted that large financial institutions were "too-big-to-fail" until the 2008 crisis took hold. The prevailing philosophy among central bankers was that markets would discipline leading institutions as shareholders and some creditors suffered losses and managers were removed. But as we learned the hard way, market discipline is not enough; some institutions are "too big to fail," and by the time they reach that point they have piled up massive excess debt on the public and seriously weakened the credit structure.

This does not mean that markets do not work, any more than it means that only markets work. The challenge is to strike the right balance in financial markets between entrepreneurial drive and fiduciary responsibility. By its very nature, enforcement of the fiduciary role in our financial system must fall chiefly on the government. Financial institutions will always push risk taking. When they innovate profitably, competitors will imitate; there is no copyright or patent on most financial innovation. Therefore, firms often seek profits through new trading techniques and new ways of increasing leverage, and seek growth through acquisition and diversification. It is therefore the job of government to set prudent rules for financial behavior.

Recent events have taught us that financial conglomerates are very difficult to manage effectively. More than that, financial consolidation will continue to undermine competition in financial markets. Leading conglomerates already control huge shares in key market sectors. They are deeply engaged in all sides of the market at the same time—on the sell side as dealers and underwriters, on the buy side as institutional investors and portfolio managers, and on both sides as financial advisers.

Diversified financial firms that engage in proprietary trading are rife with conflicts of interest. In this typically highly leveraged activity, they garner information from their huge volume of client activity, insights to which other market participants are not privy. It is a kind of inside information. Moreover, many financial holding companies house deposit institutions and benefit from the association with the deposit facility when they carry on proprietary trading. Again, the recent financial crisis revealed fissures in the system.

Greater financial concentration will significantly impede the marketability of securities. With fewer market makers, dealers, and underwriters, financing costs will increase and spreads for securities traded in the market will widen.

Another serious consequence of financial concentration is volatility. The greater the concentration in financial markets, the greater the swings in financial asset prices. The lack of diversity within markets will bring with it sharp shifts in market prices. As noticeable in recent years, this will become a global phenomenon. Financial conglomerates already have global reach. They are interconnected through myriad transactions. Opinions on markets are transmitted with the speed of light. As fewer and fewer participants dominate financial markets, prices will become more volatile. This, in turn, will call into question even the best quoted prices of the most credit-worthy obligations. Oligopoly in finance corrodes the operation of markets. With few market makers and investments held in a diminishing number of institutions, what happens when an investor group wants to liquidate? To whom does it sell?

Yet another damaging effect of financial consolidation, the most important of all, is its role in pushing our political economy away from economic democracy, whatever its imperfections. In an economy with a highly concentrated financial sector, the government will remain a powerful force in the allocation of credit, as shown by the 2008 crisis.

9

A Meeting with Margaret Thatcher

U.S. presidents and other heads of state too often sideline economic affairs when their attention is demanded elsewhere. Diplomacy, wars, and scandals are typical reasons. More than that, some leaders don't value high-level economic advice. President Herbert Hoover considered himself an economist of sorts, and spurned the counsel of leading experts. President Ronald Reagan was so confident in the wisdom of supply-side theory that he considered shutting down the Council of Economic Advisers and rarely conferred with his treasury secretary, Donald Regan.

I met several U.S. presidents: LBJ, Nixon, Ford, Carter, Reagan, and Clinton.[1] I also had two lengthy, meaningful meetings with two heads of state: Israeli Prime Minister Shimon Peres and British Prime Minister Margaret Thatcher. Peres was born in Poland, the son of a merchant and

---

[1] I have never been affiliated with either of the two major U.S. political parties. I did, however, actively support Senator Bill Bradley (D-NJ) in his bid for the 2000 presidential nomination.

© The Author(s) 2016
H. Kaufman, *Tectonic Shifts in Financial Markets*,
DOI 10.1007/978-3-319-48387-0_9

grandson of a rabbi. He moved with his family to Tel Aviv, Palestine, at age eleven, and two years later helped found a kibbutz. Politically active by his early twenties, he was jailed for scouting sites for future Jewish settlements in the Negev military zone. Peres was appointed deputy director of defense in 1952 and then director-general—playing a key role in the 1956 Suez Crisis—from 1953 to 1959. He served in the Knesset almost continuously from 1959 to 2007, and completed two terms as Israel's prime minister (Sept. 1984–Oct. 1986 and Nov. 1995–June 1996), one as interim prime minister (April–June 1977), and one as president (July 2007–July 2014), as well as minister of foreign affairs, defense, transportation, and finance at various times.

In the summer of 1986, my friend Haim Ben-Shahar (former president of Tel Aviv University) arranged for the two of us, along with my wife, Elaine, to join Prime Minister Peres at his residence in Jerusalem. It was right after the Sabbath on a Saturday, and we spent several hours together. The discussion wasn't confined to economics and finance; far from it. I should not have been surprised by the range of the Prime Minister's knowledge, given that by then he already had written several of the eleven books he eventually completed on history, politics, and biography. Still, his erudition was impressive.

My meeting with Prime Minister Margaret Thatcher was arranged by Gordon Pepper, a senior partner of the London firm Greenwell & Company, a dealer in government securities. He was quite knowledgeable about U.K. monetary and fiscal matters. In one of his meetings with the Prime Minister, my name came up, and she expressed an interest in seeing me. And so early in her term, Gordon and I presented ourselves at 10 Downing Street for a private meeting with the Prime Minister.

I knew that Mrs. Thatcher's rise to the pinnacle of British politics had been unprecedented. Her father had been a grocer and devout Wesleyan Methodist in Grantham, Lincolnshire, in southwestern England. A brilliant student, Margaret Roberts earned a B.S. in chemistry in 1947, the year after—and strongly influenced by—the recent publication of Friedrich von Hayek's *The Road to Serfdom*. After serving as president of the Oxford University Conservative Association, Thatcher was elected to Parliament (for Finchley) in 1959, and by 1975 has risen to become leader of the Conservative Party and the highest ranking woman in modern British politics. Her election as Prime Minister followed four years later.

It was a dire time to take office. Crippling strikes had turned the previous winter into a "Winter of Discontent." More broadly, the nation had been in and out of recession and was plagued with double-digit inflation for years (necessitating a £2.3 billion IMF loan in 1976). Since 1950, the U.K. had seen the percentage of its manufacturing work force shrink from nearly 50 percent to 30 percent. "Thatcherism"—much like "Reaganism" across the pond—sought to weaken the power of national regulation and labor unions while placing greater emphasis on monetary policy. The prime minister raised interest rates to wring out inflation and privatized most state-owned enterprises. In the near term, unemployment soared as briskly as Thatcher's approval ratings plummeted, but the Iron Lady stood fast. She was reelected twice and served as Prime Minister until 1990.

When we met, Mrs. Thatcher's attentiveness and quickness of mind impressed me immediately. She never wandered off the two topics she wanted to explore with me: targeting the growth of money supply as a means of stabilizing economic growth, and the desirability of inflation-indexed government bonds.

The prime minister was a confirmed monetarist. By the time we met, the definition of money already had been broadened in the U.S. and the U.K. from the narrow concept of demand deposits and currency in circulation to include quite a few other elements. In England, the favored target was M3, comprised of notes and currency in circulation with the public as well as all sterling deposits held by U.K. residents in both the private and public sectors. Because Mrs. Thatcher favored the removal of what was called the "corset" on bank lending, she hoped that a correct gauge of money supply could be adopted, one that would facilitate the efficient allocation of credit through a market-determined process.

More than that, she was concerned about the impact of money supply on England's international financial position. She combined a deep passion for the subject with a level of knowledge that I have seldom if ever seen in other heads of state. I encountered this again while reading her memoir, *The Downing Street Years*. In this illustrative passage, Prime Minister Thatcher discusses monetary policy and international trade:

> Either one chooses to hold an exchange rate to a particular level, whatever monetary policy is need to maintain that rate. Or one sets a monetary target, allowing the exchange rate to be determined by market forces. It is, therefore, quite impossible to control both the exchange rate *and* monetary policy.
>
> A free exchange rate, however, is fundamentally *influenced* by monetary policy. The reason is simple. If a lot more pounds are put into circulation, then the value of the pound will tend to fall—just as a glut of strawberries

will cause their value to go down. So a falling pound may indicate that monetary policy has been too loose.

But it may not. There are many factors other than the money supply which have a great influence on a free exchange rate. The most important of these are international capital flows. If a country reforms its tax, regulatory and trade union arrangements so that its after-tax rate of return on capital rises well above that of other countries, then there will be a net inflow of capital and its currency will be in considerable demand. Under a free exchange rate, it would appreciate. But this would not be a sign of monetary stringency: indeed, as in Britain in 1987 to mid-1988, a high exchange rate may well be associated with a considerable monetary expansion. (Thatcher 1993, pp. 689–690)

It is, unfortunately, difficult to imagine a U.S. President discussing economic matters with such sophistication and clarity.

I explained to the Prime Minister that an effective money supply target approach was out of reach. To be sure, Paul Volcker had suddenly switched to monetarism in October 1979, but he had done so as shock therapy, not as a long-term strategy. Too many structural changes in the credit market, I continued, made it increasingly difficult to define the money supply precisely. From my perspective, the financial markets were evolving into a framework in which money mattered but credit counted. Relentless financial innovation was expanding the marketplace and running ahead of official controls. As everyone later came to understand, securitization was sweeping the mortgage market. New credit instruments, especially derivatives, also were expanding the boundaries of credit. Computers allowed for the more intensive use of economic and credit data, which boosted trading activity, and *seemed* to reduce risk taking—all of which also contributed to the growth of credit.

In this new world of finance, I suggested to Mrs. Thatcher, the very concept of liquidity was changing rapidly, and with it the possibility of money supply targeting. Liquidity had been an asset-based concept based on the cash and near-term maturity securities in a portfolio (plus, for a business, the liquidity of receivables). Now, the concept of liquidity was tilting to the liability side of the balance sheet, especially for corporations and some financial institutions. Rather than assets, the primary source of liquidity now was seen as access to borrowing. This was increasingly true for individuals as well, who were relying more and more on credit card lines and home equity as potential sources of funds.

Yet another obstacle to an effective money supply target, I continued, was the rapid globalization of financial markets, with London itself playing a key role in the process. But while tightening the money supply might well restrain credit market participants confined to the domestic credit market, it would have little effect on those with access to credit internationally. The rapid growth of the Euro dollar market at the time was a case in point.

In retrospect, I should have added another point. For money supply targeting to succeed, it would require a highly diversified institutional structure in which large financial institutions did not dominate. In that kind of system, firms that did well would prosper and those that did not would fail. Conversely, in a highly concentrated structure dominated by too-big-to-fail institutions, only the smaller institutions would be allowed to fail, even if they took on less risk than the giants. A central bank cannot enforce the role of financial institutions as guardians of credit while simultaneously sheltering those institutions under a protective umbrella.

When the discussion turned to the issuance of inflation-indexed government bonds—that is, bonds that would provide a rate of return adjusted to the price index—I sensed that the Mrs. Thatcher had had many discussions with her close advisors about the subject and was leaning toward taking the step. Again, she displayed sophisticated reasoning. To begin with, she suggested, inflation-indexed bonds would shift the inflation risk from investors to the government. This was desirable, according to the Prime Minister, because the government was better able to bear the inflationary burden. This was based on the assumption that taxes are paid in nominal income that increases with inflation.

The Prime Minister also was attracted to inflation-linked bonds because they were likely to reduce interest rate costs and thus lessen the burden of government finance for taxpayers. Many academic economists also were attracted to inflation-indexed bonds because their price movements could reliably signal inflation expectations. Market participants and policymakers alike would find that useful.

In spite of this reasoning, I did not support the idea of government inflation-indexed bonds then, and still don't today. A society's most effective inflation deterrent is to experience the pain of spiraling prices and keep that memory alive. Ironically, automatically indexing bonds—or wages, or any other prices—to the inflation rate is a good way to almost guarantee unacceptable levels of inflation. More than that, because the government has far greater capacity to issue indexed bonds than the private sector, it risks precisely the kind of impoverishment (through large deficits) that Mrs. Thatcher was committed to avoiding.

But my views on the matter did not prevail. In 1981, the United Kingdom became the first developed economy in the world to issue inflation-linked obligations. The United States followed in 1997, with Treasury Inflation-Protected Securities (TIPS). Some other nations did the same, including Canada, Sweden, France and Italy. But indexed bonds never became a major source of government debt. In the United Kingdom, they presently account for a small percent of outstanding borrowing. Nor do they seem to be a reliable indicator of inflationary expectations.

There is an addendum to my meeting with Mrs. Thatcher. Gordon Pepper was among the prime minister's advisors who strongly supported the idea of issuing inflation index-linked bonds. He seemed to have

Fig. 9.1 Bank of England one penny check from index-linked Treasury bond

savored the victory. To my surprise, he purchased in my name a 1 pound index-linked Treasury bond that began to generate periodic interest checks from the Bank of England—in the amount of one penny! Where could I possibly cash such a check? No bank would bother, even though the creditor was none other than the Bank of England. So I decided to go to the top. I had that opportunity during one of the annual meetings of the IMF-World Bank in Washington, D.C., that was attended by Gordon Leigh-Pemberton, then governor of the Bank of England. I had invited to him a dinner hosted by Salomon Brothers. In my remarks that night, I asked the governor to come to the podium, where I presented him with a few of the one-penny checks. True to his institution's good name, he paid me. I had to promise that I would surrender my one-pound obligation.

10

Michael Milken: Moving Junk Bonds to Prominence

Michael Milken was a pivotal figure in late-twentieth-century bond markets. He unearthed a slumbering junk bond market and catapulted it to the forefront of the credit markets. In the process, he encouraged many bond market participants to embrace higher risk. The debt instruments he packaged and sold through Drexel Burnham Lambert helped fuel a wave of leveraged buyouts and other corporate takeover gambits, including several major deals put together by Kohlberg Kravis Roberts in the late 1980s. KKR found that negotiation with a "highly confident" letter from Drexel in hand—in which Milken offered strong assurances he would underwrite a deal—was a powerful bargaining chip. Milken's below-investment-grade bonds also were embraced by many small- and medium-sized firms hungry for growth capital as well as by stalwart institutional investors. Mr. Milken and Drexel made billions of dollars in profits before the wunderkind investor was indicted and sent to prison.

© The Author(s) 2016
H. Kaufman, *Tectonic Shifts in Financial Markets*,
DOI 10.1007/978-3-319-48387-0_10

I didn't know Mike Milken personally, but was well aware of his activities in the bond markets of the 1980s. And although I spoke with him only once, it was a conversation of some consequence.

After I left Salomon Brothers in 1988, I set up my own New York City-based investment management firm, Henry Kaufman & Company. Within the first year, a friend of mine suggested that I approach Drexel about managing a $500 million high-grade, closed-end corporate bond fund. Drexel was willing to underwrite the fund and bring it to market. It was clear to me that, for Drexel, the deal would help them establish a reputation for making markets in all sorts of credit, not just low-quality obligations. Given my well-known conservative market views, an association with me would help Drexel at a time when it was coming under increasing scrutiny by financial regulators. For my part, a successful flotation would have generated annual income of $3 million for a number of years.

Milken, a native Californian, graduated from Berkeley with highest honors in 1968 before moving on to complete an MBA at the University of Pennsylvania's Wharton School. While at Berkeley, he encountered the writings of W. Braddock Hickman, a former president of the Federal Reserve Bank of Cleveland, particularly his book *Corporate Bond Quality and Investor Experience* (1958). Hickman's dense analysis contained an insight that profoundly influenced Milken and served as the core of what would become his spectacularly lucrative and influential early career. According to Hickman, markets and credit ratings agencies tended to undervalue low-grade bonds. Even when losses from the outright default of some "junk" bonds were factored in, the bonds were still a bargain, given their total returns. In other words, he believed that junk bonds were underrated and underpriced. This offered a great opportunity for Milken to arbitrage the junk bond market.

Milken, of course, did not invent the high yield bond market. As Hickman had noted, such securities were hardly new. As recently as the 1970s, prominent firms including LTV, Pan Am, Zapata Corporation, and Fuqua Industries issued low-grade bonds. But Milken's advocacy encouraged legions of investors to purchase junk bonds, which became acceptable with institutions such as insurance companies, pension funds, mutual funds, and savings and loan associations. At the same time, Drexel Burnham Lambert, where Milken held a senior position, acted as underwriter for junk bonds. It made a secondary market for them, thus providing some liquidity for junk bond investors.

After Milken convinced Drexel to let him open an office in Los Angeles in 1978, his junk bond underwriting took off. During the superheated 1980s, when hostile takeovers, leveraged buyouts, and other battles for corporate control became popular, Milken offered corporate raiders and others a means to raise enormous quantities of capital in short order. During his most profitable years in the late 1980s, Milken earned total annual commissions of roughly half a billion dollars a year, an industry record.

According to one of Milken's former partners, SEC investigators had been suspicious of the rising star since the start of his career. But it was the indictment of inside trader Ivan Boesky in 1987 that turned the tables for Milken. Boesky, to reduce the charges he faced, agreed to wear a wire and in other ways cooperate with authorities. Among those he named for insider trading and other securities violations was Michael Milken. The investigation took two years to unfold, with future New York Mayor Rudolph Giuliani, then U.S. Attorney for the Southern District of New York, joining the fray in an effort, in part, to build his reputation as a tough prosecutor and his political fortunes. Giuliani took the unusual step of deploying RICO, the Racketeering Influenced and Corrupt Organizations Act—which had been fashioned as a weapon to fight organized crime—against Milken, Drexel, and other alleged Wall Street inside traders, claiming that their interconnected network represented a form of racketeering.

Still, Milken's fate was far from decided in 1988, when I was about to sign the Drexel corporate bond fund documents and my secretary told me that Michael Milken was calling from the West Coast. He had heard about the pending deal and asked that we get together to talk. When I explained that I was scheduled to fly to Japan to address a meeting of Japanese financial leaders and meet with several important clients, Milken suggested that I stop over in California for a brief chat on my way to Japan. Among other things, he wanted to discuss the differences in our views of market conditions and financial behavior. But it was impossible for me to adjust my schedule. He ended the conversation by saying, "Henry, it's wonderful that we are going to be doing business together."

The comment wedged in my mind, and dogged me during my entire trip to Japan. To be sure, the high-grade corporate bond fund was a worthwhile and certainly legitimate venture. But I worried about being associated with Milken—about "doing business together." Promptly on my return from Japan, against the advice of several close associates whose judgement I regarded highly, I cancelled the offering.

***

The junk bond market totaled an estimated $6 billion in 1970, the year Milken started to work at Drexel Burnham, and reached $210 billion when he left in 1989. While there have been quite a few mishaps in this market since that time, the junk bond market continued to burgeon, increasing in size during periods of monetary ease and stumbling sharply when credit availability has contracted. In 1988, only 12 percent of the total value of outstanding corporate bonds was below investment grade; by the end of 2014, the figure had climbed to 23 percent. Moreover, this market has been the most rapidly expanding component within outstanding corporate bonds.

The government also did its part in fostering the rapid expansion of junk bonds. One of its actions permitted savings and loan associations, whose investments had been confined to primarily finance home mortgages, to invest in junk bonds. On the surface, this decision to allow portfolio liberalization was extremely appealing to many managers of S&L portfolios. The yield on junk bonds was generally higher than the rate of return from mortgage obligations. Moreover, the cost of the transaction and of servicing the two obligations strongly favored junk bonds. (Junk bonds require no real servicing cost.) At first blush, the credit risk in junk bonds was mitigated by the liquidity provided in the secondary market; and the "sell side" analysis on junk bonds often gave additional comfort to investors.

Milken ultimately pleaded guilty to several securities and tax violations, such as failing to disclose the true owner of a stock, rather than to insider trading, as was popularly believed. Although sentenced to a decade in prison, he ultimately served only twenty-two months. A prostate cancer survivor, he became the leading private benefactor of prostate cancer research, and also founded a think tank devoted to economics in Santa Monica, the Milken Institute.

Mike Milken's impact on financial markets has been underrated. He influenced its participants to become much more entrepreneurial—to take more risks as borrowers and as money managers. That influence has endured through financial cycles, including the 2008 financial debacle. Of course, the weakening of the credit structure has complicated the Federal Reserve's job of assessing risk and forced it to enlarge its role as lender of last resort.

Apart from my encounter with Milken, I had become increasingly concerned about the growing prominence of junk bond finance in the 1970s and 1980s. Several partners at Salomon were eager to move the firm aggressively into that market—a strategy I opposed. I was concerned such a move would erode the firm's reputation, and had observed that Salomon's involvement with low-grade bonds had too often lacked due diligence. It was a form of undue risk, along with others, that contributed to my decision to leave the firm in 1988, a few years before the firm was fined $290 million for submitting false (multiple) bids for Treasury Bonds and was taken over by Travelers Group.

11

Financial Crises and Regulatory Reform

In the United States, meaningful financial reform has tended to be crisis-driven. That is an unfortunate fact, for several reasons. It means that our regulatory system has been defined and redefined under extreme rather than normal conditions. It means that financial regulation is more reactive than proactive. And it means that we must endure serious dysfunction, if not a major calamity, before fixing problems—financial excesses that typically have been recognized and acknowledged long before the crisis hits.

Many believe that financial and business cycles certainly are an inescapable characteristic of capitalism. (They are also endemic to socialism, but for different reasons—namely, gross misallocation of resources by the central government, along with the usual exogenous factors such as energy prices, weather, and war.) But are crises, not just cycles, also inevitable in market-based economies? Many theorists have said so, from Karl

© The Author(s) 2016
H. Kaufman, *Tectonic Shifts in Financial Markets*,
DOI 10.1007/978-3-319-48387-0_11

Marx to Hyman Minsky. Marx, of course, was convinced that capitalism would destroy itself by wantonly exploiting workers, leading to revolution and socialism. Minsky—a modern economist whom I had the pleasure of meeting on quite a few occasions and whose work was underappreciated prior to his death two decades ago—theorized that stable economic periods contain the seeds of overoptimism, which lead to overinvestment, looser credit, and eventually overspeculation, followed by a reversing trigger (which some now call a "Minsky moment") and downward panic.

The historical record in the U.S. shows that virtually every generation has suffered through a significant financial crisis for a long as we have been a nation. In the nineteenth century, they struck in 1819, 1837, 1857, 1873, and 1893. In the twentieth century, there were crises in 1907, 1929, 1966, 1970, 1987, 2000, and 2008. It is no coincidence that two of the worst financial crises (1929 and 2008) also spawned two of the twentieth century's most important waves of financial reform: the New Deal banking and securities legislation of the 1930s, and the Dodd-Frank Wall Street Reform and Consumer Protection Act of 2010. Those two financial regulatory overhauls were crisis-driven.

A brief review of these two waves of financial regulatory reform—their aims, policies, and outcomes—shows that financial reform has focused on a core set of perennial issues: first, financial concentration; second, abuse of credit; third; fiduciary responsibility; fourth, stability; and fifth, structural changes that outpace the efforts of monetary policy. We still haven't gotten it quite right. It is difficult to get it right through a political process during the super-heated atmosphere of crisis. Meanwhile, like our political process, our monetary authorities too often respond only after major problems have set in.

***

Wall Street had been controversial in American culture from the beginning. Traders of commodities and securities for many decades traded on street corners or in coffee shops, but eventually moved inside in present-day lower Manhattan. Most Americans, especially farmers—who comprised the vast majority of the population in the nineteenth century—distrusted securities traders, seeing them as "parasites" who profited off transactions rather than real work. Few understood that a developing economy required well-functioning financial services in order to mobilize capital.

The U.S. financial system was far from a "system" in the nineteenth century. The First and Second Banks of the United States—which were proto central banks—operated only for a total of forty years (1791–1811 and 1816–1836, respectively). Banks were free to print their own currencies, which literally thousands did, and not required to hold a state charter. The result was an economy with lots of liquidity sloshing around, much of it of dubious quality. The economy continued to grow robustly, but bank failures, counterfeiting, and various forms of financial fraud were epidemic.

In the early twentieth century, some states took steps to rein in the worst abuses by enacting so-called "blue sky" laws—measures that, for example, required the registration of securities, or the licensing of securities traders, or the issuance of financial statements by publicly traded companies. Meanwhile, some states began to erect firewalls between different kinds of financial institutions. New York led the way in 1905 after a highly-publicized scandal involving the insurance industry. The empire state prohibited life insurance companies from investing in collateral trust bonds or corporate stocks, and from underwriting securities. Within three years, seventeen states had similar laws on the books.

These were important steps toward greater transparency, but by this time stability, fiduciary responsibility, and structural changes—most notably financial concentration—were becoming acute. It was the age of finance capitalism, when J. P. Morgan and other Wall Street investment houses were mobilizing capital on a massive scale to finance railroads and industrial corporations. There were halting steps toward reform. But major change proved impossible without a major crisis.

In late 1912 and early 1913, House Committee on Banking and Currency hearings (named for Louisiana Democrat Arsène Pujo) conducted a series of investigations of the so-called "money trust" in America. The Pujo investigations yielded some eye-opening revelations about financial concentration and influence. For example, three financial institutions—J. P. Morgan & Co., First National Bank of New York, and National City Bank of New York, together with the two trust companies they controlled, Guaranty Trust and Bankers Trust—comprised a powerful "inner group" in investment banking. The giants exercised control over not only investment banking but much of the economy, according to the subcommittee's major report. They did this by, among other things, sitting on the boards of the companies they financed, holding their deposits, and holding large shares of other financial institutions such as trusts and insurance companies, as well as non-financial institutions such as railroads and manufacturing firms. The investigators documented that 180 inner-circle directors and bankers sat on the boards of 341 corporations (financial and non-financial) valued at some $25 billion, which, they concluded, "has resulted in great and rapidly growing concentration in the control of money and credit in the hands of these few men."

Even though the Committee failed to prove any kind of conspiracy or even that investment banking was failing to supply the capital needs of a thriving economy, the legislators recommended a sweeping agenda of reforms, including state incorporation, federal supervision, and prohibiting interstate corporations from designating a sole private fiscal agent or from even depositing their funds in private banks. To help separate different kinds of financial institutions, the Committee proposed to bar national banks from the securities business, and their officers and directors from participating in syndicates and trusts. There were many other provisions as well, nearly two dozen in all.

But Congress balked. The nation's lawmakers, startled though some were by Pujo Committee revelations, were not prepared to dramatically expand federal powers into the private domain, banking or otherwise. On April 7, 1913, Congress voted not to enact any of the Committee's recommendations. Along with fears of government encroachment, many lawmakers (especially Republicans) objected to the Committee's methods. Then, as now, widespread financial concentration in the absence of a major crisis was not enough to spur meaningful reform.

Even so, two major economic measures soon enacted were strongly influenced by the Pujo Committee's work: the Federal Reserve Act (December 23, 1913) and the Clayton Antitrust Act (October 15, 1914). One of the key reasons the Federal Reserve System was designed around twelve regional banks was to diminish the relative power of banks in the Northeast. More than that, the public–private mix built into its governance structure (with relatively greater public power than its two predecessor Banks of the United States) was intended as a check on purely private interests. For its part, the Clayton Act prohibited interlocking directorships among large banks, common carriers, and trust companies, and forbade corporations from owning stock in other corporations "where the effect of such acquisition was to substantially lessen competition."

The Great Crash of 1929 and the onset of the Great Depression were a crisis severe enough to compel major reform. Even though economic historians now place most of the blame for the Great Depression on adherence to the gold standard, in the early 1930s experts and laymen alike blamed Wall Street. On the eve of the Roosevelt administration's economic reforms, then, American banking was thinly regulated, fragmented, and opaque. Deposit insurance was localized and haphazard. Membership in the Federal Reserve System was optional. Commercial and investment banking often were conducted by the same institutions. Securities trading, meanwhile, had been criticized for decades for a host of problems: over-speculation, the concentration of power, conflicts of interest (with other financial institutions and with client firms), fraud, and lack of public disclosure. Bank and securities regulation was a hodge-podge of state blue sky laws that by and large lacked meaningful enforcement powers. These laments were hardly new, but the crisis of the Great Depression and the Pecora hearings in the early 1930s gave them a new urgency.

Roosevelt's Administration enacted three major banking and securities laws within its first eighteen months (some, it should be noted, against the wishes of the president). The centerpiece of New Deal banking reform was the Banking Act of 1933, also known as the Glass-Steagall Act. It included a number of provisions aimed at minimizing or eliminating conflicts of interest. Its main thrust was to separate commercial banking (by institutions that accepted deposits and issued loans) from investment banking (whose practitioners originated and distributed securities). Not only were single institutions prohibited from engaging in both activities, but their directors and officers were banned from interlocking directorships.

In short order, commercial banks divested investment banking functions, while most investment banks remained in that business. Another key provision of Glass-Steagall was deposit insurance. The newly-created Federal Deposit Insurance Corporation was a government-owned corporation that operated as an independent agency. Member banks had to meet certain guidelines, and the FDIC also was empowered to supervise non-member state banks. One of the most urgent problems the FDIC was designed to address was bank runs, and indeed after its establishment the runs ceased and a massive tide of depositor withdrawals was reversed as Americans regained confidence that a bank was a better place for their savings than a mattress. Originally established as a temporary measure, FDIC was made permanent by the Banking Act of 1935, which also raised the level of insured funds to $5000.

The 1933 law also prohibited commercial banks from paying interest on demand deposits (checking accounts) and set maximum interest rates on time deposits. This provision was designed to discourage banks from taking excessive risks in the face of pricing competition. It also grew out of the belief that competitive interest payments had drained deposits from the country districts into the speculative security markets during the 1920s. (As we will see, interest rate controls were one of the first elements of Glass-Steagall to be dismantled.) For the first time, the federal government was regulating commercial banking (beyond postal laws).

As for investment banking, the new watchword was disclosure. So much of what had gone wrong in the Great Bull Market, according to policymakers, had to do with corporations, investment banks, and brokerages either hiding or being blissfully unaware or uninterested in the underlying fundamentals of securities they were trading. As one observer noted at the height of the boom, some corporations had begun to market shares of stock like bars of soap or other commodities.

Little wonder, then, that the Securities Act (1933) went by the popular name the "truth-in-securities" act. In essence, the new law federalized the blue sky laws. New securities (but not outstanding ones) had to be registered with the Federal Trade Commission. Issuers of new securities were required to publish detailed financial prospectuses, and to register the new offerings twenty days before trading commenced. There were penalties for non-compliance.

Reinforcing and complementing the Securities Act was the third major banking and securities law passed in the first fifteen months of the New Deal: the Securities and Exchange Act (1934), which established the Securities and Exchange Commission. (To this day, the SEC is Wall Street's chief regulating body.) The SEC supervised the secondary market, including securities trades at physical exchanges and electronically. All firms with publicly traded securities now had to issue annual reports and quarterly earnings statements. They had to disclose major shareholders (who held 10 percent or more). The SEC also regulated exchanges, including practices such as short selling, and took over the new securities registration process from the FTC.

The nation's central bank—still scarcely a generation old—garnered new powers in the early New Deal. In combination with the 1933 banking law, the Banking Act of 1935 expanded the powers and flexibility of the Federal Reserve Bank and renamed and restructured it. The central bank became the Board of Governors of the Federal Reserve, with the Secretary of the Treasury and the Comptroller of the Currency no longer members. Replacing the Open Market Policy Conference (created in 1930) comprised of a representative from each branch, the new Federal Open Market Committee was comprised of Fed Board members plus the regional bank presidents. The Fed was given increased latitude in making loans to member banks and in backing up Federal Reserve notes and deposits. It was empowered to alter reserve requirements, to set maximum interest on time deposits, and to examine member banks. Under the new Fed it became harder to charter a new bank, for regulators believed the nation would do better with fewer banks of sounder quality.

***

These were the key components of a regulatory system that would endure in large measure for more than half a century. For the first few decades of this regime, the U.S. economy was relatively stable and prosperous, banking was a reliable if staid profession, and Wall Street investing was considered an avocation for the wealthy. By the 1970s and 1980s, however, structural changes and macroeconomic forces were putting new pressures on banking and finance. Stagflation put home buying out of reach for millions of Americans. Banks wanted to compete across state lines and (led by Citibank, as noted above) to offer new products such as negotiable certificates of deposit. Merrill Lynch and some other brokerages were popularizing stock investing among the middle class, while Fidelity and its cousins popularized mutual fund investing. Bit by bit, financial institutions were allowed to offer new products and compete in new markets.

The Savings and Loan debacle of the mid-1980s and early 1990s set off warning signals, though not loud enough to inspire major regulatory reform. Even though nearly a third of the nation's 3200 or so "thrifts" collapsed during this crisis, costing taxpayers something on the order of $132 billion, many experts blamed high inflation for causing the crisis— by driving the rates at which banks could borrow to well above the interest they were collecting from many borrowers. There is truth to this piece of the story, but it ignores the additional profound impact of financial deregulation in opening the door for S&Ls to offer higher returns on new products, and in allowing them to disguise—and therefore compound—their losses through junk bond financing and lax oversight.

All five historical targets of financial reform—financial concentration, abuse of credit, fiduciary responsibility, stability, and structural change—were abundantly present in the thrift crisis. Yet the general trend toward deregulation accelerated, culminating in the Gramm-Leach-Bliley (or Financial Services Modernization) Act of 1999. By striking down the 1933 Glass-Steagall Act's prohibitions against diversification and conflicts of interest ("simultaneous service by any officer, director, or employee of a securities firm as an officer, director, or employee of any member bank"), Gramm-Leach-Bliley effectively ended nearly seven decades of government financial oversight.

The hundreds of billions of dollars lost to the Enron-era scandals (see Chap. 12) also failed to trigger regulatory overhaul. It is revealing that in his thorough dissection of the Enron episode, Harvard Business School professor Malcolm S. Salter places greater responsibility on the credit rating agencies for the debacle than on the three federal agencies charged with overseeing company operations: the SEC, FERC (the Federal Energy Regulatory Commission), and the CFTC (Commodities Futures Trading Commission). According to Salter, those three bodies were hobbled by "gaps and overlaps in regulatory jurisdiction" and "weak review systems," and were often simply outwitted by Enron's hard-driving and often dishonest executives. "Enron's executives," he concludes, "were a bright, creative, aggressive lot. A patchwork regulatory system overseen by lenient public watchdogs was not sufficient to contain them. The watchdogs communicated inefficiently, had little time and inclination to adequately review public filings, and, perhaps most important, were inclined to take Enron at its word" (Salter 2008, p. 238).

As for the credit rating agencies, Congressional gears began to turn, but—in the absence of a major systemic crisis—they ground too slowly. Senate hearings in 2002, followed by House hearings in 2003, 2004, and 2005, yielded no real reforms. In 2008, the House and Senate launched another round of hearings. Those, of course, were overtaken by much larger events.

The U.S. government's official commission on the crisis estimated total domestic household losses at $11 trillion as of 2011. If non-U.S. costs are factored in—the crisis ricocheted through the Eurozone and contributed to a global slowdown—total losses are incalculably greater. Two years of intensive Congressional investigation and negotiation yielded the Dodd-Frank Wall Street Reform and Consumer Protection Act, signed into law by President Obama in July 2010. On the face of it, Dodd-Frank's passage was a regulatory milestone. Its key provisions are obvious outgrowths of the 2008 crisis—attempts to prevent a recurrence or, if that should happen, manage it better. Dodd-Frank, in other words, is designed to apply lessons from the greatest financial and economic crisis since the Great Depression.

One cluster of provisions is aimed at insuring greater economic stability through closer monitoring and reporting of financial markets and institutions. Another set is designed to manage the orderly liquidation of assets when financial institutions fail. Other measures centralize regulatory powers in an effort to avoid gaps and redundancies in official oversight (of the sort that enabled Enron). Some track and report on hedge funds, credit default swaps, credit derivatives, and other major markets in the so-called "shadow banking" sector. There are new investor and consumer protections, and new forms of oversight for credit ratings agencies. Dodd-Frank also reaches into financial institutions by trying to improve corporate governance and place some limits on executive compensation. At 383,013 words in its original incarnation—amendments have made it even longer—the legislation appears monumental.

Not surprisingly, Dodd-Frank has attracted plenty of critics, especially among those brought under closer scrutiny and among philosophical opponents of government regulation, who claim it will stifle entrepreneurship and erode American competitiveness. Earlier, I discussed what I see as two of Dodd-Frank's greatest shortcomings: its failure to meaningfully address financial concentration (The Bigness Crisis, Chap. 8); and its unwelcomed consequences for Federal Reserve independence (The Politicizing of the Fed, Chap. 13). Here are some of my additional concerns.

The length of the legislation is a clue to the first. Dodd-Frank is so long and complicated that both compliance and enforcement are difficult. (By way of contrast, the Declaration of Independence is some 1,300 words long, the U.S. Constitution, including all twenty-seven Amendments, 7,818 words long. The Ten Commandments are 179 words.) In effect, Dodd-Frank's verbosity says to regulators and the regulated alike: Here, you figure it out, and if things go wrong Congress will hold you responsible. That is hardly a formula for accountability or success. The law's complexity also has made it prone to endless jiggering and fine tuning, especially by its opponents. Some have claimed that, under the well-funded lobbying pressure from Wall Street, Dodd-Frank will die a proverbial death of a thousand cuts.

To help insure greater financial stability, Dodd-Frank established the Financial Stability Oversight Council (FSOC). It is charged with identifying risk to the financial stability of the U.S., promoting market discipline, and responding to emerging stability threats. Its voting members are the Secretary of the Treasury, who serves as the chairperson, the chairman of the Fed, and the heads of all the federal regulatory bodies, along with an independent member with insurance expertise. At first glance, this all sounds very reasonable. But can this diverse group make effective, timely decisions, since—with the exception of the chairman and the head of the Fed—all serve diverse constituencies? The only member of FSOC with broad responsibility for maintaining financial stability is the chairman of the Federal Reserve. But under Council's structure, the Fed chairman has only one vote.

Another concern I have about a component of Dodd-Frank pertains to the new Office of Financial Research (OFR), an independent adjunct to FSOC that reports to the secretary of the treasury. Its director is appointed by the president. Richard Berner, a former colleague of mine at Salomon Brothers, now holds that position. The Office of Financial Research is charged with, among other things, monitoring market developments and financial stability, evaluating macro prudential policy tools, advancing data standards, and addressing data gaps. Its work thus far has provided considerable insight into the operation of financial markets. For example, the OFR's study "Asset Management and Financial Stability" revealed high concentration in this sector and the risks associated with that concentration. Will the Office of Financial Stability be able to maintain its objectivity? Major financial institutions that may be adversely affected by its research findings are bound to exert political pressure.

The Dodd-Frank legislation also requires each too-big-to-fail institution to create an officially sanctioned living will—a document detailing how the institution would dissolve if it got into serious financial difficulty. This approach is based on the dubious assumption that the existence of a living will would calm markets if a big institution totters. I doubt that would happen. Even a rumor that a living will has been activated will inspire market participants to quickly sever their relationships with an institution in trouble, thus roiling the markets. Any institution deemed too-big-to-fail to begin with is by nature going to have sprawling financial connections around the globe.

Another problem with Dodd-Frank's living will provision (and general approach to financial concentration) is that it enshrines too-big-to-fail institutions in a special category, in effect transforming them into financial public utilities. Breaking up financial conglomerates into their constituent parts (investment banking, commercial banking, consumer finance, asset management, and so on) would make them easier to manage, easier to regulate, and probably more efficient. More than that, the sum of their parts very likely is worth more than their valuation as a diversified whole. This could make them targets for takeover, although the regulatory complexities of such a deal seem daunting. Several non-financial corporations (such as GE and Metropolitan Life) have downsized in order to remove themselves from the too-big-to-fail category. It is revealing that other financial institutions have not done the same, especially given the likely financial payoff. I suspect one reason is that board members and senior managers of these huge conglomerates are unwilling to vacate their lofty perches in the financial markets, even though holding on to their seats may not be in the best interest of their stockholders.

A broader perspective on the legislation suggests that it will come to possess nowhere near the historical impact of New Deal financial legislation. Too many of the fundamental vulnerabilities in financial institutions and markets remain essentially intact. The so-called Volcker Rule provision, designed to restrict proprietary trading by commercial banks, was delayed for years, weakened (collateralized debt obligations were exempted, for example), and as of now still exempts certain kinds of so-called "legacy covered funds." Similarly, as this book goes to press half a dozen years after the legislation's passage, news media report that Wall Street bankers *might* face pay restrictions from a Dodd-Frank-based "proposal" that could limit bonuses. According to the *Wall Street Journal*, "The rules would require big financial firms to defer payment of at least half of executive's bonuses for up to four years, a year longer than what is common industry practice" ("Tough Rules" 2016). This is hardly a meaningful reform.

In the immediate wake of the shattering events of 2007 and 2008, the Obama Administration squandered a rare opportunity to fundamentally revamp the financial sector. Even though Republicans in both houses were opposed, public sentiment was running strong, with some vocally "occupying" Wall Street. But the President focused on other matters, and relied too heavily on many of the same Washington and Wall Street insiders who had helped create the crisis in the first place (Suskind 2012). A half-dozen years after 2008, the question remains: Where will the second great financial crisis take American capitalism?

12

The Present Value of Financial History

In one sense, we all rely on history every day in almost everything we do—because we employ knowledge of the near-, medium-, or long-term past to understand and decide our actions. History is memory, and memory is much of what makes us human. But there is a big difference between informally recalling what has happened and systematically studying and analyzing it. It is no coincidence that dictators devote a lot of effort to destroying (think of George Orwell's novel 1984 or the Mao's "Red Guard") or completely rewriting the history of their dominions.

Ignorance of history has two main dimensions. One is refusing to believe it matters. The other is believing it matters but learning the wrong historical lessons. The way around both is to take the study of history seriously. Few of us, of course, have the time to study history rigorously, but plenty of expert advice is available. As in other fields of formal knowledge, in the study of history there are best practices. For business in particular, there are business history consulting firms and

© The Author(s) 2016
H. Kaufman, *Tectonic Shifts in Financial Markets*,
DOI 10.1007/978-3-319-48387-0_12

many careful studies of corporations, industries, and national economies, published and (for internal use) unpublished. A group of business school professors currently is dedicated to deploying historical methodologies to better understand management, leadership, entrepreneurship, corporate governance and social responsibility, and related fields (Bucheli and Wadhwani 2015).

Institutions (including firms) and their leaders can benefit enormously from a serious interrogation not only of their own histories but the larger forces that have buffeted them over time. One of the key insights to emerge from such studies is how certain practices that originated for very good reason tend to outlast their usefulness over time, to the point where the institution eventually forgets why it started doing something in the first place. The behavior has become "normalized" to the point where its reason for being is taken for granted rather than questioned periodically. Consider this observation by the venerable historian of technology, Elting Morison, about British efforts during the Second World War to improve the efficiency of some light artillery that was originally commissioned as early as the Boer War (1899–1902):

> [I]t was felt that the rapidity of fire could be increased. A time-motion expert was, therefore, called in to suggest ways to simplify the firing procedures. He watched one of the gun crews of five men at practice in the field for some time. Puzzled by certain aspects of the procedures, he took some slow-motion pictures of the soldiers performing the loading, aiming, and firing routines.
>
> When he ran these pictures over once or twice, he noticed something that appeared odd to him. A moment before the firing, two members of the gun crew ceased all activity and came to attention for a three-second interval extending throughout the discharge of the gun. He summoned an old colonel

of artillery, showed him the pictures, and pointed out this strange behavior. What, he asked the colonel, did it mean. The colonel, too, was puzzled. He asked to see the pictures again. "Ah," he said when the performance was over. "I have it. They are holding the horses." (Morison 1966, pp. 17–18)

Financial history is a branch of business and economic history. It focuses on topics such as the development of financial markets and institutions, central banking, stock exchanges, financial regulation, and—a perennially popular topic—the history of financial bubbles, panics, and crashes. There are professional journals devoted to financial history, and a major museum on Wall Street in New York, the Museum of American Finance. I've tried to support the field through the Museum and by endowing chaired professorships and fellowships in the United States and Israel.

In spite of all these efforts, there is reason for considerable pessimism about the importance of history in business and finance. Many studies report shockingly low levels of knowledge among both U.S. school children and the general public about economics, markets, and finance—a problem that Commerce Secretary Luther Hodges dubbed "economic illiteracy" back in 1962[1] ("Hodges Plans" 1962). Of course, college students are an important target cohort, especially those who aspire to careers in business or finance. But there, too, the news is not good. For a generation or more, our business schools have been turning out technicians rather than broadly educated graduates. Almost without exception, undergraduate and MBA courses focus on skill-building rather than larger considerations of the role of business in political, social, and historical perspective. Marketers learn how to effectively place products; supply

---

[1] The Council for Economic Education has been tracking and battling the problem for decades. There has been an uptick on public school teaching about economics and finance since the 2008 crisis (Sovich 2016).

chain and operations management majors learn logistics; and organizational behavior majors how to keep workers satisfied and productive. For their part, finance majors learn the intricacies of their craft with little or no consideration of its crucial social or historical roles. To be sure, most programs require a business ethics course. But ghettoizing ethical considerations into a single course or two rather than infusing the topic into the whole curriculum can send the wrong message. In general, today's business school curricula includes a large dose of number crunching.

Any kind of historical perspective is painfully lacking. When I attended New York University in the 1950s, many of the nation's better college programs routinely required courses in business history, economic history, and the history of economic thought. The number of such offerings has declined markedly as schools of business administration in particular have come to see history as an unnecessary luxury or a frivolous (albeit interesting) pursuit. The masters of technique turned out by our business schools are ill-equipped to understand change over time or how broad political, social, and economic developments impinge on financial markets, and vice versa. I know of no top-rated MBA program in the country that now requires students to complete one or more courses in financial, economic, or business history.

In short, our financial leaders need broad horizons. Financial crises are rife with valuable lessons. One need not delve into the deep past—to, say, the Dutch tulip craze of 1637 or the South Sea Bubble of 1720. Many times in the twentieth century, credit over expanded, private actors overstepped legal and ethical boundaries, and regulators grappled with problems that students of the 2008 crisis would find quite familiar. Every financial crisis is unique, yet the commonalities far outweigh the differences. In their historical amnesia, financial leaders, investors, and regulators alike are squandering a valuable resource, one with very practical value.

Most importantly, our new financial leaders need to understand, deeply and convincingly, that maximizing profit is not their sole responsibility. They are also trustees of our society's credit. Deans and faculty members in our business schools must try to insure that the next generation of managers, especially those who will head leading financial institutions, bring a broad perspective to their offices. Where else if not in the university—the bastion of intellectual exploration—can we expect this to happen? Our business schools have become too much like trade schools.

Let me suggest a few lessons from financial history that have come to me as a long-time participant in financial markets and a student of financial history. There are many others. These, however, strike me as among the most notable for being regularly discovered, forgotten, rediscovered, and so on. I hope that business students and managers who are not reading this chapter somehow come to learn these lessons the easy way—that is, *before* ignorance of them exacts considerable costs.

Let's begin with one of the more well-known subjects in financial history—heroes. In finance as in other fields of history, biography remains a popular genre. We study the lives of leading figures not only for their intrinsic interest but also because we might learn something about these "greats" that might inform our own lives. It seems to me, however, that in financial history, *those who are heralded as heroes often turn out to be villains*. A few twentieth century examples illustrate the point.

Ivar Kreuger (1880–1932) was born into the family of a leading Swedish industrialist and built an even larger business empire of his own, especially in construction and match manufacturing. His position in the latter business became so dominant globally that he became renowned as "the Match King."

Kreuger also became famous for a series of financial innovations, including convertible gold debentures, American certificates (or American Depository Receipts), binary foreign exchange options, and B-shares (or dual class ownership shares). Some of Kreuger's financial instruments are still used today, and he also regularly employed off-balance-sheet entities in the style of Enron and other firms decades later. After Kreuger's death, some $250 million of the magnate's alleged $630 million proved to be fictional. The collapse of Kreuger's empire caused a financial panic in the early 1930s, especially in Sweden and the United States.

Kreuger's firms typically paid double-digit returns while in fact earning in the single digits, but only a portion of his malfeasance was the result of a so-called Ponzi scheme—a term named for one of his contemporaries, Charles Ponzi (1882–1949). Ponzi is another example of hero turned villain. With a scam involving his alleged arbitraging of postal reply coupons that he purchased in other countries, the Italian immigrant promised investors a return of 50 percent in forty-five days or 100 percent in ninety days. He paid these returns out of capital from new investors, a pyramiding concept he did not pioneer but practiced on the grandest scale to date. His scheme's collapse in mid-1920 brought down the Hanover Trust Bank of Boston, which Ponzi and his friends owned, plus three other financial institutions, and cost investors about $20 million.

Although suspicions had circulated around Kreuger and Ponzi for years, each was widely regarded as a financial genius before his downfall. Kreuger, a far more sophisticated player than Ponzi, earned millions in legitimate profits along with his ill-gotten gains. But like Ponzi he recognized the public's hunger to believe in—and profit from—extraordinary returns. In a rare moment of candor, the Match King admitted that "I've built my enterprise on the firmest ground that can be found—the foolishness of people."

Financial heroes later revealed as con men don't always thrive on foolishness; sometimes the financial establishment helps make the myth. That was the case for Enron Corporation, which evolved from a natural gas pipeline company in 1985 into an electricity supply company, high tech firm, and energy trading company with reported earnings of $100 billion in 2000. Along the way, Enron was praised widely. *Fortune* magazine ranked Enron the "most innovative" company in the U.S. every year from 1996 to 2000, the year the Harvard Business School published a highly laudatory business school teaching case about the company. Major credit rating agencies ranked Enron bonds triple A until shortly before its collapse. The company was grossly overstating earnings by sheltering liabilities in literally thousands of special purpose entities. Senior executives Kenneth Lay and Jeffrey Skilling secretly sold their Enron shares while reassuring investors of the company's soundness up until declaring massive losses in late 2001 that sent the firm into a death spiral. Investor losses from Enron's collapse were estimated at $67 billion. More than that, California residents paid more than $11 billion in artificially inflated electricity rates during a "crisis" engineered by Enron's energy traders. Enron also gave its name to an "era" because it was followed by a number of similar catastrophic corporate scandals in the early twenty-first century, including Tyco, WorldCom, Global Crossing, ImClone, Adelphia, and HealthSouth.

Financial schemers typically capitalize on periods of market enthusiasm, especially environments in which Wall Street experts claim that the old rules no longer apply. Ponzi began his scheme as the "Roaring 'Twenties" was getting underway, whereas Kreuger attracted millions of new investors during the decade's great bull market. Enron's great appeal was its claim to be turning one of the most boring industries in American history—electric power—into one of the most innovative and dynamic. It was a message many investors were primed to hear during the rising tide of business and financial deregulation in the late 1970s, 1980s, and 1990s.

That was also a period in U.S. financial history when hedge funds became popular among high-end investors. As their name implies, hedge funds promised their investors a way to minimize risk by hedging it through off-setting investments. But each deal requires a counterparty, so even though hedge funds claim to minimize or eliminate risk, they are in fact placing bets that they are better at assessing risk than their counterparties. Such claims seem all the more credible to investors when the hedge fund appears to have an edge, and in recent times their claimed advantage has come more and more in the form of sophisticated models.

In the superheated investment environment of the 1980s and 1990s, the hedge fund Long-Term Capital Management, founded in 1993 in Greenwich, Connecticut, offered seemingly unmatched brain power and sophistication. It was the creation of one of my former colleagues, John Meriwether, who had racked up an astonishing record of success as head of bond trading at Salomon before resigning amid the company's trading scandal in 1991. LTCM recruited a great deal of talent from Wall Street and academia, including former Federal Reserve Vice Chairman David W. Mullins, Jr., and two Nobel Prize-winning economists, Robert C. Merton and Myron S. Scholes, who had pioneered new methods for pricing derivatives. The firm's credentials and connections were so impressive that it raised more than $1 billion by the time it began trading in early 1994.

That year—when all bond investors on average lost money—LTCM earned a return of 28 percent, with a net to investors after management fees of 20 percent. Meriwether's letter to shareholders included an attachment by Scholes and Merton in which the two esteemed economists offered columns of precise calculations purporting to show how often the hedge fund would lose money, and by what percentages (e.g., at least 5 percent in 12 of every 100 years). As LTCM chronicler Roger Lowenstein aptly explains: "It was as if the professors had some secret knowledge or an altered view of the world, for no ordinary investor would hazard such forecasts. Most people, one hopes, know that their stocks can fall, but if asked to specify the odds, they would mostly likely blink in puzzlement" (Lowenstein 2000, p. 62).

The unpredictable storms that scuttled LTCM came in 1997, with the Asian financial contagion and the Russian government default the following year. Within a few months, LTCM lost nearly $2 billion in capital. After a buyout deal offered by Warren Buffet, Goldman Sachs, and AIG failed, the New York Federal Reserve, fearing systemic collapse, orchestrated a $3.6 billion bailout, which in effect proved to be a coordinated liquidation (by 2000). In the end, the new investors walked away with modest profits, the partners lost all their $1.9 billion, and total losses reached some $4.6 billion. The hedge fund's wunderkinds had engineered one of history's greatest financial calamities.

Another lesson from financial history is that *during boom times many market participants become convinced that the old rules no longer apply.* Many had in mind Wall Street when they referred to the 1920s as a "New Era." This New Era, one contemporary gushed, "meant permanent prosperity, an end of the old cycle of boom and bust, steady growth in the wealth and savings of the American people, [and] continuously rising stock prices." Alexander Dana Noyes, a financial columnist at the *New York Times,* was among only a handful who expressed skepticism and concern about the great bull market before the 1929 crash. He had been closely watching markets for decades, and relied "on the teaching of experience that human nature does not change and that even financial history repeats itself" (Klein 2003, pp. 22–23, 27).

Dominant attitudes during more recent financial bubbles bear an eerie similarity to the "this time is different" talk of the 1920s and many other early boom periods. Rather than the "New Era," the 1990s was dubbed a "New Economy." Rather than the automobiles and consumer durables of the 1920s or the plastics and mainframe computers of the 1960s, this time the Internet embodied most of the new glamour companies and industries. Yahoo, AOL, Netscape, Amazon and others were said to be not only capitalizing on a robust economic expansion, but also rewriting the very rules of business in the process. Traditional measures of financial performance such as ROI and price-earnings ratios increasingly were viewed as stodgy if not irrelevant in valuing companies. They applied to old "bricks and mortar" businesses. New measures like "eyeballs" and "clicks"—which measured visits from potential customers, not actual sales—helped drive up the value of many web-based companies dramatically. When James K. Glassman and Kevin A. Hassett published *Dow 36,000* in 2000—at a time when the index had only recently cracked the 10,000 mark—the book sold briskly. Soon the dot.com bubble had burst.

Not every economic or financial boom ends in panic. Bubbles remain extremely difficult to identify, at least at the time they are possibly forming. More than that, although every financial bubble is unique, *they share a common core of lax credit standards and the overexpansion of credit*. Once lenders become convinced that a "New Era" or "New Economy" has dawned, many become willing to extend credit on increasingly unrealistic terms. For their part, borrowers are all too happy to accept the liberalized terms, even without reasonable expectations they can meet their obligations.

Monetary authorities have an important role to play during strong bull markets. They *should strive to keep borrowing and lending responsibly aligned, and to rein in excesses.* Unfortunately, the historical record is littered with central bank shortcomings. Although financial markets and the economy are semi-autonomous, the former can have a powerful influence on the latter through, among other things, the wealth effect (the fact that households spend more when the prices of their key assets such as real estate and retirement savings are high). During both the dot. com bubble and bust and the housing bubble that led to the massive crisis of 2008, Alan Greenspan's Federal Reserve held back from constraining credit enough to risk throwing cold water on the economic expansions. (In the next chapter I discuss how Fed policy has become more politicized in this and other ways.) This was a long way from the days of Fed chairman William McChesney Martin, who deemed it the job of the central bank "to take away the punch bowl just as the party gets going."

It seems to me that another enduring lesson from financial history is that *the greater the intermediation in financial markets, the greater the distance between lenders and borrowers, to the peril of markets.* This dynamic was central to the sub-prime mortgage crisis, in which mortgage lenders quickly offloaded obligations to other intermediaries, who in turn repackaged and resold them, and so on. In addition, the growing quantification of financial analysis has brought with it the assumption that only data that can be counted and modeled matter. Powerful econometric tools have their benefits, but also some significant limitations that only personal contact between lenders and borrowers can address. The Bank of England's governor, Mark Carney, put it this way: "In the run-up to the crisis, banking became about banks not businesses; transactions not relations; counterparties not clients. New instruments originally designed to meet the credit and hedging needs of businesses quickly morphed into ways to amplify bets on financial outcomes" (Carney 2014).

Free societies cannot survive through brute force. They must nurture their own cultures, and continue to provide opportunities for students to reflect on their heritage and learn from recurrent patterns. Along with social and political history, economic and financial history are essential if we are to produce leaders informed enough to preserve what is best about our society and culture. As the erudite British Rabbi Jonathan Sacks reminds us, according to Moses, "[f]reedom … is won, not on the battlefield, nor in the political arena, but in the human imagination and will. To defend a land, you need an army. But to defend freedom, you need education. You need families and schools to ensure that your ideals are passed on to the next generation, and never lost, or despaired of, or obscured. The citadels of liberty are the houses of study. Its heroes are teachers, its passion is education and the life of the mind" (Sacks 2000, p. 34).

13

The Politicizing of the Fed

The U.S. Federal Reserve's record since the end of World War II has been checkered at best. Along with some significant accomplishments have come considerable shortcomings. The central bank's greatest achievements are these: First, under Paul Volcker's leadership (see Chap. 4), the Fed broke the back of the virulent inflation that had plagued the economy for a decade and a half beginning in 1965. Had prices continued their upward spiral for much longer, our economy, and possibly our very social structure, could have suffered dire consequences. Second, under Ben Bernanke, the Fed—albeit belatedly—helped ameliorate the macroeconomic impact of the 2008 financial crisis. While it is true that Greenspan's Fed policies contributed to the credit binge at the heart of the crisis, his successor acted innovatively to help ward off what likely could have morphed into a great depression. Indeed, monetary policy-makers deserve considerable credit for the fact that the U.S. hasn't suffered a major depression since the 1930s.

© The Author(s) 2016
H. Kaufman, *Tectonic Shifts in Financial Markets*,
DOI 10.1007/978-3-319-48387-0_13

There have been other achievements as well. The Fed played a key role in resolving the silver crisis in the 1970s, in mitigating debt crises in Latin America in the early 1980s, in heading off a credit crunch after the 1987 Wall Street crash, in stabilizing global credit markets during the 1997 Asian financial crisis, and in warning of systemic collapse in 1998 in the wake of the spectacular failure of the massive hedge fund, Long-Term Capital Management. Each of these monetary emergencies might have worsened considerably if not for the Fed's decisive actions.

At the same time, the Fed took far too long to respond to the inflationary buildup in the 1970s, and to the overexpansion of housing debt—particularly low-quality—throughout the subsequent decades. More broadly, the central bank has failed to set forth a philosophy or rationale for our financial system based on fundamental tenets that would improve the regulatory structure. What kind of a financial system do we really want? What should our financial institutions and markets strive to achieve? How can this be accomplished while safeguarding the public trust? Are there important distinguishing aspects between financial institutions and other private enterprises in the economy?

As a starting hypothesis, it seems uncontroversial that our complex, advanced economy requires a robust and well-integrated financial sector to intermediate the savings and investment process. Financial institutions and markets reconcile the needs of both the demanders and suppliers of funds. If we did not have an efficient financial system, the behavior of spending units and of savers would be severely limited and our economic performance would be sharply curtailed. Among other things, a well-functioning financial system should facilitate stable economic growth. In a broader sense, it should promote reasonable financial practices and curb excesses.

Some members of the financial and academic communities make an important distinction among the underlying functions of the financial system. They divide the functions into two parts: to provide a mechanism through which flow all payments; and to provide the framework through which allocating credit is efficient. This distinction is made because there is a clear need to safeguard the payments mechanism, but it is less clear that our system of credit allocation requires such safeguards. I believe, however, that in the financial world today, these functions are intertwined. A shift in attitudes over the last few decades has caused the differences between money and credit to become blurred.

Indeed, the Fed has failed to recognize on a timely basis changes in the financial structure and the implication of these changes for monetary policy. Here are some of the major structural changes.

Many traditional banks as well as other institutions engage in "spread banking," an effort through which institutions try to lock in a rate of return that exceeds the cost of their liabilities. This came to the fore when the Fed ultimately removed the interest rate ceilings on time and savings deposits and the banks moved to floating rate loans for these borrowers. The immediate impact of this practice was that it freed both borrower and lender from the early restraint imposed by the Fed. For example, in the 1970s and early 1980s, interest rates had to escalate sharply before both lender and borrower desisted. What occurred was a large run-up in interest rates, accompanied by a massive growth of debt that brought about a sharp deterioration in credit quality for both participants. The Fed failed to conceptualize what these events would do to the conduct of monetary policy.

The new banking practice raised a serious question. Should financial institutions experience the benefits and discomforts of monetary policy or should they be mere conduits that pass on the full impact of policy to households and businesses? Over the last several decades, financial institutions have increasingly become conduits. Through spread banking and other techniques, they have quickly passed on the higher cost of funds to local government, business, and household borrowers in order to protect their own profit margins. As a result, much higher interest rates have been required to achieve effective monetary restraint, more borrowers have become marginal, and the quality of debt held by financial intermediaries has deteriorated as well.

Second, the Federal Reserve failed to genuinely appreciate the significance for monetary policy of the rapid increase in the securitization of obligations—the process by which a nonmarketable asset is turned into a marketable instrument. Today, many credit instruments have been securitized, including consumer credit obligations, mortgages, higher yielding corporate bonds, and many derivative instruments. They facilitated the rapid growth of debt, a sharp falloff in the oversight of these obligations, and credit quality deterioration. Yet the general impression given for a long time by Fed officials, most notably Chairman Greenspan, was that securitization improved liquidity and that these obligations reduced the concentration of risk from a smaller group of lenders to many participatory lenders, thus diffusing the concentration of risktaking. The efficacy of that conclusion did not hold.

Third, the Fed adhered to the notion that liquidity was heavily based on the amount of short-term assets on the balance sheets of households and businesses. As noted earlier, that changed several decades ago. While households continue to include short-dated assets, they also include in their capacity to borrow the equity in their homes and their unused consumer credit lines. Business adds to their liquidity unused credit lines and an estimate of their open market borrowing capacity. This liberalization in the concept of liquidity surely contributed to credit creation beyond the expectations of the Fed.

Fourth, I have long questioned whether the Fed has been able to include in its calculations the extent to which financial institutions and markets are much more international in their activities. Funds flow from one country to another electronically with extraordinary volume, sometimes moving counter to underlying trade developments. Facilitating these international flows, large U.S. commercial banks and investment banks have built up large operations in key foreign money centers, and concurrently, foreign financial institutions are enjoying an increased presence in the United States. Today, many U.S. borrowers participate in both U.S. and foreign financial markets, and U.S. institutional investors are becoming more familiar with international opportunities.

Fifth, the opportunity for reward has carried risk. The experience of our money center banks in lending to developing countries is one example. Managing the risk of floating exchange rates in a world of 24-hour-a-day-trading is another. It is increasingly difficult to correlate all the flows of funds and assess their significance. Not surprisingly, recent investigations have revealed many illegal international transactions that the Fed and other regulatory bodies failed to uncover in a timely way, such as Libor (London Interbank Offered Rate) manipulation going back to at least the early 1990s. As a writer for the *Wall Street Journal* summarized the fallout from that "vast" scandal: "Roughly a dozen financial institutions have agreed to settle charges that their employees sought to manipulate the ubiquitous benchmark to enhance their profits, with the firms in many cases entering criminal guilty pleas and collectively paying billions of dollars in penalties." Some involved in the episode are serving prison terms (Enrich 2016).

Finally, perhaps the most significant development has been the impact on monetary policy of the concentration of financial assets in the hands of a few institutions. The Fed encouraged the removal of Glass-Steagall without appreciating the impact this would have on the conduct of future monetary policy. The huge consolidation that occurred after its removal has now created institutions that are too-big-to-fail. This and other developments have put the Federal Reserve in an extremely difficult position (on which I will elaborate later).

From my perspective, the Federal Reserve has not spoken or written enough about the role and obligations of financial institutions. Financial institutions are not just the guardian of credit, but in a broader sense, they are also the mechanism that can either strengthen or weaken a market-based society. Financial institutions should be part of a process that encourages moderate growth of debt and substantial growth of equity and ownership. To be sure, to achieve such objectives, a correct fiscal and tax structure must be in place. Substantial risktaking and entrepreneurial zeal belong properly in the world of commerce and trade, where large equity capital tends to reside, not in financial institutions that are heavily endowed with other people's money. Encouraging increased leveraging of financial institutions automatically induces greater leverage in the private sector, making it more vulnerable, more marginal, and eventually inviting government intervention. The whole process thus undermines the essence of an economic democracy.

In this regard, there are a number of unalterable facts. First, when financial institutions act with excessive entrepreneurial zeal, the immediate outcome is economic and financial exhilaration. Only later, when the loan cannot be repaid on time or the investment turns sour, are the debilitating and restrictive aspects of the excesses fully evident.

The events of recent years bring into focus the issue of the independence of the Federal Reserve. In an incisive speech before The Economic Club of New York in May of 2013, Paul Volcker, in speaking on this subject, said, "In the last analysis, independence rests on perceptions of high competence, of unquestioned integrity, of broad experience, of non-conflicted judgment and the will to act. Clear lines of accountability to the Congress and the public will need to be honored. Moreover, maintenance of independence in a democratic society ultimately depends on something beyond those institutional qualities. The Federal Reserve—any central bank—should not be asked to do too much, to undertake responsibilities that it cannot reasonably meet with the appropriately limited powers provided."

He diplomatically entitled his talk, "Central Banking at a Crossroad." I believe that the Federal Reserve has crossed the road and is now on a path to politicization from which it will be difficult to reverse. To a large extent, this reflects its own lack of strategic thinking. Because it did not oppose the huge acceleration in the concentration of financial institutions that started in the 1990s and which it actually encouraged when the financial crisis began in 2008, the Fed is now very close to managing the direction of these large financial conglomerates. Because these huge financial conglomerates are now deemed "too-big-to-fail" and their activities are difficult to monitor, Federal Reserve personnel and other official supervisory authorities now sit physically in these institutions. Some even attend the board meetings of these large institutions. What a striking difference this is from years ago, when banking regulators visited banking institutions only periodically to review their holdings and operations.

Moreover, the Federal Reserve is one of ten voting members of the Federal Supervisory Oversight Committee, which is charged with, among other things, preventing future financial mishaps. It shares that responsibility with other supervisory authorities that cover special designated sectors of the markets and therefore have limited capacity to judge the totality of risks in the financial markets. How independently will all these voting members act when they judge the state of market conditions? The oversight needed should be managed by the Fed in consultation with some of the other supervisory authorities.

The new monetary tactics pose serious risks for the Federal Reserve. Monetary theory does not address forward guidance. Explicitly, forecasting the future of business activity is unprecedented for monetary policy. This tactic might well be appropriate if the forecasts have had a high degree of accuracy. They have not. Nevertheless, market participants are virtually mesmerized by these projections. As a consequence, monetary policy is increasingly guiding the actions of our financial markets. Large financial conglomerates that are now too-big-to-fail have become financial public utilities, but other institutions will be allowed to fail. That will further increase financial concentration and intensify political scrutiny of monetary policy.

Considering all the structural changes in financial markets, domestically and internationally, it makes sense to ask: Should the central bank's structure be reformed so that it can meet contemporary challenges head on? For one thing, the Federal Reserve's geographical configuration—the placement of its twelve district banks—has been obsolete for a long time. The bank's heavy presence in the Midwest and Northeast made sense in the still mainly agricultural and newly industrializing nation of a century ago, but became anachronistic as population and economic activity burgeoned in the West and South. California—itself the world's seventh largest economy—and six additional Western states are served by a single district (or Federal Reserve) bank in San Francisco, while the entire

South is covered by just two districts and two district banks (Dallas and Atlanta). Meanwhile, as in 1913, Missouri still boasts two district banks (Kansas City and St. Louis).

Governance of today's Fed is distorted by some musty rules about Federal Open Market Committee membership and voting authority. Currently, the voting members of the FOMC are the seven Board Governors but only five of the twelve district presidents. The president of the New York Fed is a permanent member—which makes sense, given the continued importance of New York City as the key international financial center. But at any given time, seven of the other district bank presidents cannot vote. Voting rotation among the district bank presidents is rooted in historical decisions with no relevance today. Why should the presidents of the Chicago and Cleveland Fed districts act as voting members every other year while the presidents of the other nine distinct banks are voting members every third year? Are these two districts as relevant economically and financially as decades ago? Consider also where the major markets and institutions are domiciled today. Bank of America, for instance, one of the nation's largest financial institutions, moved its headquarters from San Francisco to the Richmond Federal Reserve District some time ago.

The term structure of the members of the Federal Reserve Board also needs to be re-evaluated. The fourteen-year terms of the seven Board members originally was intended to help insulate monetary policy from immediate political pressure. That is an admirable objective, yet history shows that most Fed governors do not serve out their full terms.

Another area ripe for reform is Board of Governors' compensation. According to a Reuters report, Fed chairperson Janet Yellen, whose salary is set by Congress, earns only $201,700 per annum. That is well below what at least 113 other staffers at the Fed's Washington headquarters earn per year—$246,506, on average, and $312,000 for the central bank's Inspector General (Flaherty 2014). The Governors' pay comes nowhere near the millions of dollars a year earned by many heads of private financial institutions. Yet the Fed Chairperson and Governors are entrusted with the guardianship of our financial system. As in the private sector, perhaps some salary competition among central banks will improve the situation in the U.S. It was recently reported that the new governor of the Bank of England will receive more than $1 million annually.

The Fed's legitimacy depends to a large degree on whether it can retain its independence of action. So while the compensation for public bankers should be brought closer in line with that of private bankers, their real and perceived roles must remain separate. Unfortunately, Fed officials, like many other key government officers, often move in and out of private sector financial employment during their careers. But Fed officials—or, for that matter, other individuals serving in key financial positions in the U.S. government—should be banned from going into private financial institutions for several years after leaving government service.

The Federal Reserve's founders surely would be astonished by the size and composition of the American economy today, and by the power and complexity of its central bank. While the United States economy has changed dramatically over the last century, its central bank has not kept pace. Considering all that has transpired during the Fed's more than 100-year history and the challenges confronting it, this is a timely moment to review and reform the Federal Reserve's basic responsibilities, structure, tactics, and policies. Yet, however sound the reasons for meaningful reform, the prospect touches politically sensitive nerves. The central bank has built considerable inertia over the last century. Incumbency tends to prevail. But doesn't it make more sense to undertake a serious review and restructuring of the Federal Reserve at a time of relative stability, when calmer heads are likely to prevail, instead of waiting until the next wave of financial and economic turmoil?

14

Tectonic Shifts

One of the great assets of the present day, it is often argued, is the new information revolution. The World Wide Web is only twenty years old, yet investors now have access to geometrically more information than a generation ago, as well as sophisticated new tools for modeling that information. Even so, our heavy reliance on statistics carries considerable risks, especially on the policy side. The data are rich and accessible, but how accurate and valid are they? Consider a few illustrations.

The broadest measure of American economic activity is the concept of Gross Domestic Product. First, we are given preliminary estimates. Then, a little bit later, come a series of revisions. And much later, GDP data is revised back over quite a few years. This process plainly demonstrates the weaknesses in the original figures. And, of course, GDP has many critics, most of whom focus on what the measure leaves out—including unpaid housework, child rearing, and volunteer work; negative indicators of spending (such as unemployment-driven credit card spending);

© The Author(s) 2016
H. Kaufman, *Tectonic Shifts in Financial Markets*,
DOI 10.1007/978-3-319-48387-0_14

inequality; and sustainability, to name a few. As a historian of the GDP measure put it, "Our most important performance measure says nothing about whether quality of life is improving, or even if our activities are viable. It only tells us about how much stuff was produced, and how much money exchanged hands" (Philipsen 2015, p. 4).

Productivity is another favorite measure. But as defined as real business output, this concept, too, is flawed. As Al Wojnilower has pointed out in an important memo circulated through Wall Street, this conventional productivity number fails to account for the large proportion of GDP comprised of government and non-profit activity—from education, law enforcement, and public utilities to NGOs and religious organizations. More than that, Wojnilower has noted, "Quantity is measured but quality is ignored .... Ironically when, as many believe happens in air traffic [control], passenger miles rise but personnel is reduced and services deteriorate, measures of productivity increase."

There are also problems in how we measure inflation. The Consumer Price Index, as it is now constituted, is plagued with, among other things, sampling errors, substitution bias, a market basket of new goods bias, and a quality change bias. In dissecting the latter, Martin Feldstein has written that "there is no way to know how much of each measured price increase reflects quality improvements and how much is a pure price increase" (Fullerton 1994). How much sense does it make to measure the experience of viewing a color television fifteen years ago versus a high-definition, flat-screen, plasma set today based strictly on their relative prices? In spite of all these shortcomings, inflation measures are critical in monetary policy and in the behavior of financial markets.

Yet another measure that is a staple of economic analysis, especially in forecasting, is business cycle analysis. Cyclical upswings and downswings vary widely in duration and magnitude. Yet analysts tend to look at historical, cyclical averages. The problem is that statistical averages tend to conceal significant differences among up and down cycles. Consider, for example, this simple exercise. There were eleven recessions between November 1948 and December 2007. On average, they lasted only eleven months and diminished GDP by 1.9 percent. That seems rather mild. Looking at the individual episodes, though, we see that one recession lasted eighteen months, two more endured for sixteen months each, and six of them drove down GDP by 2.4 percent or more. Those valleys are disguised by the averages.

More broadly, the prevailing analytical approach to cycles fails to capture key structural changes in business and finance and their significance. For example, the cyclical economic expansion in the 1990s was viewed by many as "the great moderation" but it was driven by enormous growth in non-financial debt. That powerful structural change was disguised amid the aggregate data on macro cycles.

Relying solely on cyclical economic analysis can lead to false expectations. In the current environment, this way of thinking could suggest that we will return to earlier "normal" patterns in the yield curve, return to monetary policy that was effective in the past, or allow market mechanisms alone to automatically adjust large distortions in the financial markets. In each of these cases, I am convinced, We Can't Go Home Again. Because profound structural changes—akin to tectonic shifts—are altering the economic and financial landscape in profound and enduring ways.

Tectonic shifts are remaking Europe. The monetary union is now comprised of twenty-eight nations with a variety of strengths and weaknesses. While the same could be said about the fifty individual states in our country, we are a single politically unified nation; Europe is not. Although our union includes some economically stumbling Greece-like states, severing them from the whole is inconceivable. In Europe, it is not out of the question. European political pluralism has contributed to its malaise. Lending and investing activity within the EU has been relatively lax. Much of the financial activity within the Eurozone has been carried out liberally, without due diligence, and guided by the false assumption that sovereign borrowings would incur minor risk. But it is highly unlikely that Europe could achieve political union any time soon. Rather, the risks are grave that the EU can continue to muddle through within its current framework.

Another tectonic shift is the likely fate of the so-called BRICs. The emerging capitalist economies of Brazil, Russia, India, China, and South Africa were long expected to expand robustly, and in the process fundamentally alter world geopolitical and economic relations. Now, their weaknesses are coming to light. Corruption, poor legal systems, enormous financial excesses, dubious economic and financial data from official sources, and underestimated dependence on the developed world are among the enervating forces at work. In some of these nations, powerful robber barons exercise undue political influence. Many have become expert at exporting and sheltering their newly amassed wealth (as known from reports of the mysterious ownership of high-end real estate in New York and London). The American robber barons of the nineteenth century, when we were still a developing nation, did no such thing; they reinvested most of their wealth in their domestic enterprises. The BRICS will no doubt regain their economic traction eventually. But it will take time and some considerable reforms of their legal, financial, and economic institutions.

In Japan, the tectonic shifts are much more subtle. The country's aging population must depend on a relatively shrinking population of wage-earners. National debt is among the highest in the world, although most of it is held domestically. Japan has yet to emerge from its so-called "Lost Two Decades," which began in the early 1990s with the collapse of a ridiculous lending binge, followed by years of government support of so-called "zombie" banks. Japan may eventually increase its military spending, which would boost economic activity. Meanwhile, Japanese ethnic and cultural hubris will continue to support its strong anti-immigration policies, which in turn will hamper economic growth.

Immigration is hardly a new issue, but it has emerged as one of the defining issues of our times. For hundreds of thousands of years, humans populated the continents through long migrations, and most premodern economies were nomadic. With the rise of the nation-state, humankind encountered its first large-scale, man-made barriers to open migration. As the economic historians Kevin H. O'Rourke and Jeffrey Williamson have documented, the wave of globalization that rose during the late nineteenth century was shattered by the First World War and the global Great Depression. One major result was a backlash against the relatively free movement of workers across national borders (O'Rourke and Williamson 1999). After welcoming immigrants for generations with this inscription by Emma Lazarus on the Statue of Liberty (dedicated 1886)—

> *Give me your tired, your poor,*
> *Your huddled masses yearning to breathe free,*
> *The wretched refuse of your teeming shore.*
> *Send these, the homeless, tempest-tossed to me,*
> *I lift my lamp beside the golden door!*

—the United States enacted severe immigration restrictions in 1924. As the latest wave of globalization brings its own stresses, we are seeing evidence of another retreat from international labor migration.

Immigration poses a special conundrum for capitalist systems. Adam Smith, the first great theorist of capitalism, was a fierce opponent of mercantilism, the system—then practiced best by the British—of controlling trade throughout the empire. Although there was little movement of non-slave labor in Smith's day, the great economist applauded migration to new colonies as a driver of economic growth. Smith wrote in *The Wealth of Nations* that "An injudicious tax offers a great temptation to smuggling," and thus advocated low tariffs. It is reasonable to assume he favored the unhindered movement of people as well as goods. He was also magnanimous toward citizens of nations and locales, declaring in *The Theory of Moral Sentiments* that "Our good-will is circumscribed by no boundary." Today's conventional thinking about capitalism's factors of production favors the free movement of capital and goods, but not labor.

Then and now, the prime mover of cross-border migration is the search for a better standard of living. Advanced communication technologies heighten the issue. The poorest societies on earth possess enough access to the Internet, television, and cell phones to witness quite clearly the vast disparity between their existence on one or two dollars a day (average per capita) and the riches of the developed world. This is a powerful motivator to migrate.

Although many of the world's poorest regions have made great strides in the last generation, thanks largely to economic globalization, the gap between rich and poor societies remains enormous. Developed nations might commit more funds to shrinking the gap, but that seems unlikely given the strains on their domestic budgets. Another approach, also unlikely, would be for the developed nations and regions to expand the boundaries of their trade and investment zones. The EU, for instance, could extend its boundaries into Northern Africa. Given the EU's aforementioned travails, however, and similar issues in other regions, *private* rather than public investment will continue to lead economic development for the foreseeable future.

The tectonic shifts I have outlined in this chapter hardly exhaust the list. They will define social, political, and diplomatic life for the foreseeable future. There is no going back. In the next chapter, I consider a number of tectonic shifts in economics and finance. Some emerged only in the last decade or so, yet already have produced profound effects. Whether they are welcomed or not, to ignore them is to stumble half-blind toward the future.

15

You Can't Go Home Again

Nostalgia has a powerful draw. Sometimes we desire to return to the magic of a youthful romance, the triumph of a winning sports play, the excitement and comradery of college life, or even the hardships and struggle that ultimately brought success. But as Thomas Wolfe portrayed vividly in his aptly named 1940 novel about small town life, *You Can't Go Home Again*. The home you leave is never the home you find upon return.

The same truism applies to economics and finance. Many aspects of earlier economic times and earlier market relations can seem wonderfully appealing. These rosy memories include the 1950s and early 1960s, when the economy grew reasonably well; when banks made loans locally and knew their borrowers personally; when mortgages were thirty-year fixed, with no variable rates, balloon payments, or other fancy business; and when the Fed's mission was monetary policy, period. The more senior

© The Author(s) 2016   **145**
H. Kaufman, *Tectonic Shifts in Financial Markets*,
DOI 10.1007/978-3-319-48387-0_15

of us recall the days when households and businesses had to work hard to get credit, and when banks were banks, insurance companies insurance companies, and so on. Banking was considered a rather leisurely profession, as reflected in the relaxed connotation of the phrase "bankers' hours." Only a generation ago, mortgage-backed securities, collateralized debt obligations, synthetic derivatives, and credit default swaps were virtually unknown, much less commonplace. And in investment banking, many-centuries-old firms that recently disappeared were still leading forces on Wall Street just a few years ago.

Should we try to return to such a world? Can we? The answer to the first question is "no" because, almost without exception, the answer to the second question is "no." We can't go home again, so we shouldn't try. The question then becomes: What are the new realities?

In U.S. financial markets, tectonic shifts have been breathtaking, their consequences only beginning to unfold, debt has been growing at a very rapid clip, not only in absolute terms but, more importantly, relative to GDP. This is a break from the early postwar period, when the two moved more or less in sync. The gap between GDP growth and increasing debt appeared in the mid-1990s, and has continued to widen ever since, even during the post-2008 Great Recession. Since then, government borrowing has been a major component of total debt; U.S. government debt now stands at 101 percent of GDP, versus 63 percent in 2007, and only 54 percent in 2000.

In contrast, household debt and state and local government debt have changed little since 2008. And yet, they remain at historically high levels. Meanwhile, borrowing by non-financial business corporations, also historically high, continues to climb; since 2008 it has risen 14 percent.

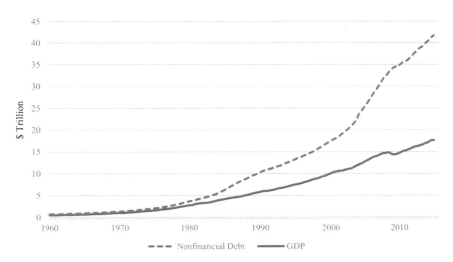

Fig. 15.1   Outstanding U.S. domestic non-financial debt and nominal GDP. *Source*: Federal Reserve

	Dec. 31, 1988	Dec. 31, 1992	Aug. 31, 1999	Dec. 31, 2014
Credit Rating:				
Aaa-A	64.95%	64.42%	52.94%	42.79%
Baa	23.47%	25.18%	22.93%	33.88%
Bb and Lower	11.58%	10.40%	24.13%	23.33%
Total	100.00%	100.00%	100.00%	100.00%

Fig. 15.2   Market value of outstanding corporate bonds classified by credit rating. *Source*: Standard & Poor's

The relative and absolute *volume* of debt are not the only issues. Equally important is the dramatically deteriorating *quality* of debt in recent decades.

Consider the following:

In the mid-1980s, sixty-one non-financial corporations were rated AAA. Today, there are only two. In 1988, 35 percent of outstanding bond debt was rated Baa or lower. That percentage jumped to 47 percent in 1999 and 57 percent in 2014.

Corporations have come to rely more and more on debt in their financing strategies. During the 1990s, total corporate debt rose $4.1 trillion,

	1990-99	2000-2007	2008-2015
Pre-Tax Profits	$ 3,878.7	$ 5,610.7	$ 9,125.4
Less:			
Taxes	$ 1,306.6	$ 1,572.1	$ 2,082.7
Dividends	$ 1,742.4	$ 2,535.9	$ 3,839.4
Plus:			
IVA	$ (16.6)	$ (159.1)	$ (97.7)
Net New Equity	$ (550.2)	$ (1,812.7)	$ (2,825.9)
Net Change in Equity	$ 262.9	$ (469.1)	$ 279.7
Net Change in Debt	$ 4,108.0	$ 6,950.2	$ 8,155.7

Fig. 15.3 Net change in equity book value and in debt of non-financial corporations, 1990–2015. *Source*: Flow of Funds Data - Q32015

compared with an increase in corporate equity of only $263 billion. And between 2000 and 2007, net equity levels actually contracted, while debt climbed another $7 trillion. Since then, equity is up $280 billion, dwarfed by an additional increase in debt of $8.2 trillion.

Many market observers point to the fact that non-financial business corporations are sitting on more than $2 trillion in liquid assets. But the analytical significance of this is overstated because this liquidity is highly concentrated. Among the 425 non-financial corporations in the S&P stock index, a mere 20 hold 61 percent of the group's total liquidity. Among state and local governments, the decline in credit quality seems to be bottoming out, although it remains well below the levels of earlier economic expansions.

For their part, household borrowers are benefitting from the liberal terms in the automobile financing market, but heavy borrowing for higher education presents a more mixed picture. With total student loans topping $1 trillion, we have to wonder how much this debt burden will restrain new household formation.

	Billions of Dollars			
	1990	2000	2008	2015 Q1
Total Domestic Nonfinancial Debt Outstanding	10,827	18,122	33,755	41,736
Household Debt	3,568	6,960	13,851	13,509
Nonfinancial Business Debt	3,774	6,579	10,688	12,178
Federal Government Debt	2,498	3,385	6,362	13,087
Local and State Governments Debt	987	1,198	2,855	2,963

	% Change Over Last Period			
	1990	2000	2008	2015 Q1
Total Domestic Nonfinancial Debt Outstanding	-	67.37%	86.27%	23.64%
Household Debt	-	95.06%	99.02%	-2.47%
Nonfinancial Business Debt	-	74.33%	62.45%	13.94%
Federal Government Debt	-	35.51%	87.93%	105.72%
Local and State Governments Debt	-	21.32%	138.37%	3.75%

	% of GDP			
	1990	2000	2008	2015 Q1
Total Domestic Nonfinancial Debt Outstanding	181.07%	176.20%	229.34%	236.26%
Household Debt	59.67%	67.67%	94.10%	76.47%
Nonfinancial Business Debt	63.11%	63.97%	72.61%	68.94%
Federal Government Debt	41.78%	32.91%	43.22%	74.08%
Local and State Governments Debt	16.51%	11.65%	19.40%	16.77%

Fig. 15.4 Composition of domestic non-financial debt outstanding for selected periods. *Source*: Federal Reserve Board of Governors, Flow of Funds

Another major shift in the American financial markets is the extraordinary increase in financial concentration. This rapid increase started in the 1990s and gained momentum during the Great Recession of the last decade. As noted in The Bigness Crisis (Chap. 8), the ten largest U.S. financial institutions now hold nearly 80 percent of all financial assets. As of 1990, there were 15,400 FDIC-insured deposit institutions in the United States. The number fell to 9,900 in 2000, 8,400 in 2008, and now stands at only 6,300.

The U.S. asset management industry manages the allocation of about $53 trillion in financial assets. The ten largest firms in that sector accounted for fully a third of the total.

In mutual funds, the U.S. Government Office of Financial Research reports that at the start of 2013, a literal handful—the five largest—mutual fund complexes managed half the nation's mutual fund assets, valued at $6.6 trillion. The top twenty-five firms controlled three quarters of total mutual fund assets.

As noted earlier, the number of independent securities firms on Wall Street has contracted sharply. Only two prominent ones remain—Goldman Sachs and Morgan Stanley—but even they operate under the Bank Holding Company structure.

Acute financial concentration has and will continue to have far-reaching implications. To begin with, it is transforming the competitive dynamics within financial markets. The decline in the number of dealers, underwriters, and market makers is widening the spreads for securities and driving up financing costs.

More than that, as markets become more concentrated and less diverse, they will become more prone to sharp shifts. Asset prices will swing more frequently and more broadly, calling into question even the most reliable prices quoted for the soundest equity and most credit-worthy debt. This won't be confined to U.S. financial markets, but rather will become an increasingly international phenomenon, thanks to the global reach of the top financial conglomerates and the near instantaneous transmission of market information. *The fewer the key market makers, the less effective the operation of market forces.*

Another consequence is that the role of the central bank will continue to be highly visible and active as compared with the more modest role it played in the early postwar years. This will reflect the fact that, in essence, the traditional sources of market liquidity have diminished, and as a consequence, the central bank will be forced to be a front-line liquidity buffer. Let me state the problem from a somewhat different perspective. The volume of outstanding marketable securities has increased dramatically over the last few decades. But the making of markets has become increasingly concentrated. This is unhealthy for markets as they function as a source of liquidity. As a consequence, the role of the state as a provider of liquidity has increased significantly. We saw this vividly in the crisis of 2008.

Growing financial concentration is a key driver of a significant shift in monetary policy. In the post-World War II era, the Federal Reserve typically ameliorated business recessions through a combination of lower interest rates and lower reserve requirements. Those traditional measures were not enough in 2008. Because of high financial concentration, the potential failure of any of the largest financial conglomerates posed systemic risks. Monetary policy therefore became even more decisive in crisis management. And the Fed will not be able to retreat from its new, highly visible role.

The Federal Reserve actually backed itself into this position by failing to understand the monetary policy implications of structural change in financial markets. The central bank didn't give serious attention to securitized financial assets or financial derivatives until those instruments were well entrenched in the markets. The Fed readily accepted the removal of the Glass-Steagall Act. It did not make clear to Congress how financial concentration would impede the functioning of financial markets and traditional monetary policy. It also failed to clarify for legislators that provisions of the Dodd-Frank Act would entangle the Fed in the oversight and management of institutions that Congress deemed too-big-to-fail, a role that reaches beyond central banking's classical mandate. It is rather ironic that the shortcomings of Fed policy, especially during the last few decades, have propelled the central bank into public prominence and policy dominance.

Another consequence of the changing structure of financial markets is that the Fed will make little progress to achieving monetary normalization although market participants believe that this is achievable. They are encouraged by the end of quantitative easing. They hope that gradual increases in short-term interest rates eventually will bring the structure of interest rates more into alignment with past patterns, and that the Fed will make meaningful progress in reducing the size of its balance sheet.

And yet, it is highly questionable whether the Fed will meaningfully reduce its balance sheet in the near term or, under certain circumstances, the long term. By holding securities until they mature or selling them into the market, the central bank is in effect exercising a form of monetary tightening through reducing bank reserves. When the Fed executes reverse repurchase agreements, bank reserves also contract; but the unwinding of the repos causes bank reserves to rise again. In order for the Fed to sell securities outright, and thus reduce bank reserves and the availability of credit in the market, we will need to see significant increases in the underlying inflation rate. If and when the Fed begins to liquidate securities from its portfolio, it will be worth observing whether the securities sold cover the entire maturity structure or are focused on the shorter or longer term. The latter would suggest that the Fed is still involved in influencing the shape of the yield curve.

A further consequence is that the Federal Reserve will most likely pursue an interventionist policy that will reach beyond quantitative easing. Stress testing the large institutions that are deemed too-big-to-fail is just one outward manifestation of official supervisory activism. Another is the big step-up that thus far has gone unnoticed. Today, official supervisory personnel are physically domiciled on the premises of large institutions to monitor their activities. Some are even present at board meetings.

What is yet to come is a policy of selective credit intervention, whereby the Fed will deploy direct guidance and vigorous moral suasion in an effort to head off widespread market speculation. There probably is no alternative to this action when monetary policy needs to tighten. This is because, in a financial world where large institutions are not allowed to fail, traditional monetary restraint will fall heavily on the other (smaller) institutions. Some will fail, but their assets will be absorbed by others, boosting financial concentration even more. In this way selective credit market intervention will serve as a kind of credit creation circuit-breaker, somewhat similar to the interest rate ceilings on time and savings deposits in place during the early decades of the post-World War II period.

Considering this increasingly active role of the Fed, it is quite likely that its quasi-political independence will be challenged across the political spectrum. As I noted in an earlier chapter, pressures will mount to reform the structure of the Fed including, among other things, the composition of the Fed Board, the composition of the Federal Open Market Committee, and the election of regional Fed bank presidents.

At the same time large institutional asset managers already under scrutiny by the official regulators will quickly discover that the size of their holdings hinders active portfolio management, which in turn will encourage more official regulatory oversight. As noted earlier, consider what would happen if several large institutions wanted to liquidate very large holdings of equity or debt at the same time. (Perhaps they had reached negative market views nearly simultaneously.) Who would step up as a capable buyer?

One of the unrecognized aspects of the current structure of our financial markets is that it lacks enough capacity to finance a meaningful increase in economic activity. Considering the new financial framework, it is difficult to envision a credit market that can sustain significantly higher interest rates. In addition, the demanders of credit in the private sector already are burdened by high debt levels (from a cyclical perspective); so higher interest rates would pose a serious refinancing problem. As noted earlier, corporate credit quality since the end of the Great Recession has not improved. With profit growth likely to slow, while mergers continue at high levels, we will see corporate debt substituted more and more for equity.

The household sector does not have the capacity to lift its borrowings by post-cyclical proportions. As shown in Fig. 15.3, household borrowings are already high. A cyclical rise in household debt going forward would produce a new round of credit quality deterioration, unless household income rose sharply—an unlikely prospect.

Only the U.S. government has the capacity to increase its borrowings meaningfully. Its debt as a percent of GDP is not threatening its credit rating. The average maturity of the U.S. Government publicly owned debt is seventy months, as compared with fewer than forty-nine months in 2009. The U.S. dollar's role as the key reserve currency is unlikely to be challenged in the foreseeable future, and therefore will not be a threat to the government's borrowing capacity. Those who favor a neutral fiscal posture are confronted with a serious conundrum. How can the economy continue to grow if private sector borrowers do not have the capacity to lift their indebtedness to achieve real GDP growth of 2.5–3 percent while maintaining a neutral fiscal policy posture? The unalterable fact is that without credit growth, there cannot be economic growth. To be sure, increasing fiscal stimulus will require some political maneuvering. Conservatives will favor tax cuts while liberals will prefer an increase in governmental spending. That combination of actions is hardly new.

Interest rate patterns cannot escape the influence of evolving financial markets and the influences of official policies on them. As noted earlier, the drop in market liquidity and the decline in credit quality will contribute to significant volatility, which in turn will prompt the Fed to stabilize conditions through open market admonitions, through open market purchases along the entire yield curve, and through selective credit allocation. Eventually, a high concentration of investment funds in relatively large institutions may also compel the Federal Reserve to purchase a much broader range of assets to stabilize conditions.

These developments—the new structure of the financial markets and the official policy responses to them—raise the rather difficult question of what interest rates will look like over the longer term. This pattern, known as the secular trend, stretches over a long period, perhaps decades, during which interest rates sweep upward or downward. These broad movements are clearly discernible even though they may be interrupted by fluctuations ranging from less than a year to several years.

Figures 15.5 and 15.6 illustrate these swings. They update data in my 1986 book and are based on the pioneering work of Sidney Homer. The magnitude of the secular swings in interest rates since World War II has been unprecedented. Prior to World War II, secular interest rate movements—from peak to trough or vice versa—ranged from 23 percent to 54 percent in secular bull markets, and from 31 percent to 65 percent in bear markets. In sharp contrast, the extraordinary secular bear market that began in 1945 endured for thirty-five years and raised long-term interest rates from a low of 2.45 percent to a high of 13.6 percent. (Please note the data are annual averages.) Thereafter, the secular bull market that began in 1981, and is thus incomplete, has endured for 35 years, with yields falling from 13.6 percent to 2.2 percent.

As for the future secular pattern in interest rates, what I stated in my 1986 book is as true today as it was then: "Currently assessing a shift in the secular direction of interest rates is by far the most complex feat in interest rate forecasting. There is nothing that is more complicated and

	Annual Average Yields				Change		Duration
	Peak	Trough	Peak		Basis		in
Governments:	%	%	%		Points	%	Years
1798	7.56						
1810		5.82			-174	-23	12
1814			7.64		182	31	4
					8		16
1814	7.64						
1824		4.25			-339	-44	10
1842			6.07		182	43	18
					-157		28
1842	6.07						
1853		4.02			-205	-34	11
1861			6.45		243	60	8
					38		19
Corporates:							
1861	6.45						
1899		3.2			-325	-50	38
1920			5.27		207	65	21
					-118		59
1920	5.27						
1946		2.45			-282	-54	26
1981			13.57		1112	454	35
					830		61
Governments:							
1981	13.45						
2015		2.84	NA		-1061	-79	34

Fig. 15.5 Secular swings in long-term U.S. interest rates. *Source*: Homer and Sylla 2005; updated with recent data

difficult to evaluate in all of investment and portfolio analysis." Very often, rising interest rates have been associated with wars and rising inflation, while falling interest rates have been correlated with longer periods of reasonable economic stability as well as with depression and deflation.

But that is not the complete story. There are many other elements to consider, including: changes in financial regulations, governmental stabilization policies, financial innovations, and international linkages. I still believe that making predictions about a change in the secular trend of interest rates is like standing in the middle of a street block trying to anticipate what is coming around the corner. Even so, market partici-

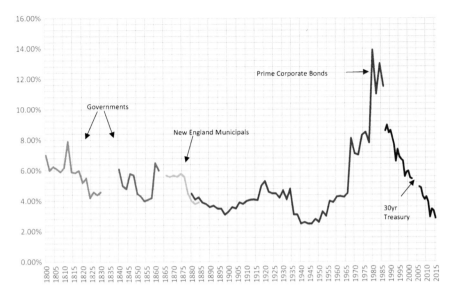

Fig. 15.6   Long-term U.S. high-grade bonds, 1800–2015. *Source*: Kaufman 1986, supplemented with recent data

pants who focus entirely on cyclical elements, which is very typical, while ignoring more secular rate trends do so at their peril.

With these caveats in mind, here are a few thoughts about the next secular rise in interest rates. The secular decline in long-term government bond yields is over. It ended last year when the yield on those bonds fell to 2.1 percent (Wigglesworth 2016). From here on, the key issue is really whether markets will experience another interest rate swing that will mirror the spectacular increase from 1946 to 1981. I doubt that very much, given recent profound changes in our financial markets and in official policies. Major financial institutions have lost much of their power to engage aggressively in financing and investing transactions. They have become financial public institutions, much like utilities, that conduct business under the tight scrutiny of official supervisory authorities. Drastic alternations in these arrangements would, of course, have a significant impact on interest rate movements. Also, as noted earlier, key private-sector demanders of credit do not have the financial capacity to be aggressive borrowers because their credit worthiness is not strong enough. And as also noted earlier, the decline in market liquidity will lead to growing financial volatility that will encourage the Fed to attempt to anticipate extreme swings through open market purchases along the entire yield curve and dampen them through selective credit allocation directives. Indeed, the high concentration of investments in relatively few very large institutions may well require the Federal Reserve to purchase a much broader range of assets to stabilize market conditions.

Recent events in the American economy and in financial markets have been described by some as "the new normal." It is a label that does not fit the circumstances. If this is "the new normal," what was the "old normal?" Was there ever an old normal? Was the old normal typified by the events in the 1950s, when the financial institutions were highly liquid, business corporations pursued conservative financing practices, and household borrowings were moderate? Or was the old normal reflected in the events of the 1960s and 1970s, when inflation gathered momentum, interest rates reached new peaks, and markets and the economy seemed to lose their moorings? Or can it be claimed that the old normal was embodied in the period from the 1980s to 2007, one highlighted by excessive financial entrepreneurship and unprecedented credit creation that eventually undermined economic activity? If there is anything like a period of economic normality, it comes out of a statistical construct in which economic and financial data are cyclically aggregated and averaged to some standard called a norm. It is an illusory comfort to assume that such constructs can serve a useful purpose.

It is far better to recognize that we will not be able to go home again. To better understand the new economic realities, we need ambitious new modes of economic and financial analysis. During the Enlightenment, Adam Smith perceived the essential workings of capitalist economies in connection with human nature and social organization. In the Age of Revolution, Karl Marx shed penetrating light on capitalism's dark underbelly—also through sweeping analysis across time and across many societies. John Maynard Keynes ushered in a revolutionary way of thinking about the relationship between markets and the state during modern capitalism's great twentieth century crisis. Frederick von Hayek and Milton Friedman, in the tradition of Smith, showed us the genius of price signaling and market coordination. But the economies and financial systems those brilliant analysts understood so well have continued to evolve, as capitalism remains ever restless. Our continued heavy reliance in recent decades on quantitative economic analysis that often is based on questionable historical data is unlikely to steer us out of the current quagmire. In the tradition of earlier great political economists, our great need today is for a much more encompassing approach to understanding the interrelationships between financial and economic behavior.

In this book and in this chapter, I have explored a number of what I have deemed tectonic shifts in financial markets—that is, broad transformations brought about by structural, technological, political, and market forces. These transformations, while hardly permanent, will leave their imprint on global business and finance for many years to come. The list of tectonic shifts below is far from exhaustive but recounts in summary form eight that I believe are among the most important—and the most often overlooked.

- The concept of financial liquidity, as understood in the private sector, has shifted away from one that was heavily asset-based on the balance sheets of households and business to one based on ready access to credit. Although households continue to include short-dated assets, they now also include their capacity to borrow on the equity in their homes and their unused consumer credit lines. For their part, businesses now include in their liquidity unused credit lines and an estimate of their open market borrowing capacity.

- The reality of a financial asset's marketability has shifted and no longer is well understood. The underlying assumption that market participants will always offer a viable trading price no longer holds as it once did. Rather, because private sector credit quality has deteriorated over the last few decades, there is now underlying uncertainty about how much can be traded *at a specific price over various phases of an interest rate cycle.*

- With the rapid growth of corporate debt alongside very limited growth of corporate equity, business creditors will experience substantial losses during future financial crises. Junk bond investments have fared quite well up to now, but that will not continue as corporate credit quality continues to decline.

- Large financial institutions cannot escape from being too-big-to-fail. They hold a huge share of private savings and temporary funds. As a consequence, they are well on their way to becoming financial public utilities, regardless of the political leanings of the government in power.

- Large institutional investors cannot initiate huge shifts in their portfolio preferences without disrupting financial markets. At best, they can make only incremental shifts. Imagine what would happen, for instance, if two or three large institutions decided to reduce their portfolio risks by 20 percent. Who would be there to buy, and at what price?

- In highly concentrated financial markets, only participants with a small market share can capture extremely large gains. And of course they can also suffer very large losses that in some instances could lead to failure.
- When financial assets in the private sector are highly concentrated, only the central bank can meaningfully supply liquidity. This makes it impossible to reduce the central bank's high visibility or its crucial role as a financial stabilizer.
- Ironically, the Federal Reserve has vaulted itself into a position of high prominence not because of its achievements but because of its shortcomings.

Too much has changed for us to return to a financial world much like that of the early postwar decades. It is far better to recognize that we will not be able to go home again. To better understand the new economic realities, we need ambitious new modes of economic and financial analysis. Our continued heavy reliance in recent decades on quantitative analytical techniques that often are based on questionable data is unlikely to steer us out of the current quagmire. Our great need today is for a much more encompassing approach to understanding the interrelationships between financial and economic behavior.

Bibliography

Adams, Richard V., et al., eds. 1994. *The Art of Monetary Policy*. Armonk, NY: M.E. Sharpe.

Aliber, Robert Z., and Charles P. Kindleberger. 2015. *Manias, Panics, and Crashes: A History of Financial Crises*. 7th ed. New York: Palgrave Macmillan.

Ball, Laurence. "The Fed and Lehman Brothers." Paper presented at the National Bureau of Economic Research Conference on Monetary Economics, July 14, 2016.

Bernanke, Ben S., ed. 2000. *Essays on the Great Depression*. Princeton: Princeton University Press.

Bernanke, Ben S. 2015. *The Courage to Act: A Memoir of a Crisis and Its Aftermath*. New York: W.W. Norton & Company.

Bremner, Robert P. 2004. *Chairman of the Fed: William McChesney Martin Jr., and the Creation of the Modern American Financial System*. New Haven: Yale University Press.

Bucheli, Marcelo, and Daniel Wadhwani, eds. 2015. *Organizations in Time: History, Theory, Methods*. Oxford: Oxford University Press.

Burns, Arthur F. "The Anguish of Central Banking." The 1979 Per Jacobsson Lecture, Belgrade, Yugoslavia, September 30, 1979.

"Business Day." *New York Times*, January 15, 1995.

Calomiris, Charles W. 2000. *U.S. Bank Deregulation in Historical Perspective*. Cambridge, UK: Cambridge University Press.

© The Author(s) 2016
H. Kaufman, *Tectonic Shifts in Financial Markets*,
DOI 10.1007/978-3-319-48387-0

Carney, Mark. "Inclusive Capitalism: Creating a Sense of the Systemic." Address delivered at the Conference on Inclusive Capitalism, London, May 27, 2014.

Conti-Brown, Peter. 2016. *The Power and Independence of the Federal Reserve.* Princeton: Princeton University Press.

Dunn, Donald H. 1975. *Ponzi: The Incredible True Story of the King of Financial Cons.* New York: Broadway Books.

Eichengreen, Barry J. 1992. *Golden Fetters: The Gold Standard and the Great Depression, 1919-1939.* New York: Oxford University Press.

Eichengreen, Barry J. 2015. *Hall of Mirrors: The Great Depression, the Great Recession, and the Uses and Misuses of History.* New York: Oxford University Press.

Enrich, David. "Six Ex-Brokers Acquitted of Libor Rigging in London." *Wall Street Journal*, January 27, 2016.

Fairlie, Robert W., et al. "2015, The Kauffman Index, Startup Activity, National Trends." Ewing Marion Kauffman Foundation, June 2015.

Financial Crisis Inquiry Commission. *The Financial Crisis Inquiry Report.* Washington, D.C.: U.S. Government Printing Office, January 2011.

Flaherty, Michael. "At Least 113 Staffers at U.S. Fed Earn More Than Yellen." *Reuters*, October 17, 2014.

Friedman, Walter A. 2014. *Fortune Tellers: The Story of America's First Economic Forecasters.* Princeton: Princeton University Press.

Fullerton, Don. "Tax Policy." In *American Economic Policy in the 1980s*, edited by Martin Feldstein, 165–233. Chicago: University of Chicago Press, 1994.

Greenspan, Alan. 2007. *The Age of Turbulence: Adventures in a New World.* New York: Penguin Press.

Guill, Gene D. "Bankers Trust and the Birth of Modern Risk Management." The Wharton School, University of Pennsylvania, March 2009.

Hickman, W. Braddock. 1958. *Corporate Bond Quality and Investor Experience.* Princeton: Princeton University Press.

Hill, Claire A., and Richard W. Painter. 2015. *Better Bankers, Better Banks: Promoting Good Business through Contractual Commitment.* Chicago: University of Chicago Press.

"Hodges Plans 62 Drive On 'Economic Illiteracy'." *New York Times*, February 10, 1962.

Homer, Sidney, and Richard Sylla. 2005. *A History of Interest Rates.* 5th ed. Hoboken, NJ: Wiley.

Kaufman, Henry. 1986. *Interest Rates, the Markets, and the New Financial World.* New York: Times Books.

Kaufman, Henry. 2000. *On Money and Markets: A Wall Street Memoir.* New York: McGraw-Hill.

Kaufman, Henry. 2009. *The Road to Financial Reformation: Warnings, Consequences, Reforms.* Hoboken, NJ: John Wiley & Sons, Inc.

Klein, Maury. 2003. *Rainbow's End: The Crash of 1929.* New York: Oxford University Press.

Krantz, Matt. "6% of Companies Make 50% of U.S. Profit." *USA Today*, March 2, 2016.

Liaquat, Ahamed. 2009. *Lords of Finance: The Bankers Who Broke the World.* New York: Penguin Press.

Lowenstein, Roger. 2000. *When Genius Failed: The Rise and Fall of Long-Term Capital Management.* New York: Random House.

Lowenstein, Roger. 2015. *America's Bank: The Epic Struggle to Create the Federal Reserve.* New York: Penguin Press.

"Martin Compares Present Boom To Period Before the Depression." *New York Times*, June 2, 1965.

Mayer, Martin. 1993. *Nightmare on Wall Street: Salomon Brothers and the Corruption of the Marketplace.* New York: Simon & Schuster.

McClannahan, Ben. "Banks' Post-Crisis Legal Costs Hit £200bn." *Financial Times*, June 8, 2015.

McCormick, Roger. "Conduct Becoming Costly." *Financial World*, June/July 2015.

McDonald, Lawrence G., and Patrick Robinson. 2009. *A Colossal Failure of Common Sense: The Incredible Inside Story of the Collapse of Lehman Brothers.* New York: Crown Business.

Minsky, Hyman P. 1986. *Stabilizing an Unstable Economy.* New Haven: Yale University Press.

Morison, Elting E. 1966. *Men, Machines, and Modern Times.* Cambridge, MA: The MIT Press.

O'Rourke, Kevin H., and Jeffrey G. Williamson. 1999. *Globalization and History: The Evolution of a Nineteenth-Century Atlantic Economy.* Cambridge, MA: MIT Press.

Philipsen, Dirk. 2015. *The Little Big Number: How GDP Came to Rule the World and What to Do about It.* Princeton: Princeton University Press.

Posen, Adam S. "Big Ben: Bernanke, the Fed, and the Real Lessons of the Crisis." *Foreign Affairs* 91:1, January/February 2016, pp. 154–159.

Sacks, Jonathan. 2000. *A Letter in the Scroll: Understanding Our Jewish Identity and Exploring the Legacy of the World's Oldest Religion.* New York: Free Press.

Salter, Malcolm S. 2008. *Innovation Corrupted: The Origins and Legacy of Enron's Collapse.* Cambridge, MA: Harvard University Press.

Sanford, Charles S., Jr. "Social Contract." Address, September 1992.

Sanford, Charles S., Jr. "Financial Markets in 2020." Address, August 1993a.

Sanford, Charles S., Jr. "The Social Value of Financial Services." Address, October 1993b.

Sanford, Charles S., Jr. "Managing the Transformation of a Corporate Culture: Risks and Rewards." Address at the Wharton School, University of Pennsylvania, November 14, 1996.

Shane, Scott. 2008. *The Illusions of Entrepreneurship*. New Haven, CT: Yale University Press.

Silber, William L. 2012. *Volcker: The Triumph of Persistence*. New York: Bloomsbury Press.

Sobel, Robert. 1993. *Dangerous Dreamers: The Financial Innovators from Charles Merrill to Michael Milken*. New York: John Wiley & Sons, Inc.

Sovich, Nina. "Could You Pass Sixth-Grade Economics?" *Wall Street Journal*, March 1, 2016.

Suskind, Ron. 2012. *Confidence Men: Wall Street, Washington, and the Education of a President*. New York: Harper Perennial.

Temin, Peter. 1989. *Lessons from the Great Depression*. Cambridge, MA: MIT Press.

Thatcher, Margaret. 1993. *The Downing Street Years*. New York: HarperCollins.

"Tough Rules Threaten Banker Pay." *Wall Street Journal*, April 22, 2016.

Treaster, Joseph B. 2004. *Paul Volcker: The Making of a Financial Legend*. Hoboken, NJ: John Wiley & Sons.

Turner, Adair. 2016. *Between Debt and the Devil: Money, Credit, and Fixing Global Finance*. Princeton: Princeton University Press.

U.S. House of Representatives, Committee on Oversight and Government Reform. "Hearings on the Financial Crisis and the Role of Federal Regulator." Washington, D.C., October 23, 2008.

Vanasek, James G. "Statement of Former Chief Credit Officer/Chief Risk Officer 1999-2005." Washington Mutual Bank, Before the Senate Permanent Subcommittee on Investigations, April 13, 2010.

Volcker, Paul A. "Central Banking at a Crossroad: Remarks by Paul A. Volcker Upon Receiving the Economic Club of New York Award for Leadership Excellence." Address before the Economic Club of New York, May 29, 2013.

Wigglesworth, Robin. "Henry Kaufman says Trump will help kill 30-year bond rally." *Financial Times*, November 11, 2016.

Wolfe, Martin. 2014. *The Shifts and the Shocks: What We've Learned—and Have Still to Learn—from the Financial Crisis*. New York: Penguin Press.

Zweig, Phillip L. 1995. *Wriston: Walter Wriston, Citibank, and the Rise and Fall of American Financial Supremacy*. New York: Crown Publishers, Inc.

Index

© The Author(s) 2016
H. Kaufman, *Tectonic Shifts in Financial Markets*,
DOI 10.1007/978-3-319-48387-0